The PHRASEBOOK
SPANISH

English edition prepared by First Edition Translations Ltd,
Great Britain
Designed and produced by AA Publishing
First published in 1995 as Wat & Hoe Portugees,
© Uitgeverij Kosmos bv – Utrecht/Antwerpen
Van Dale Lexicografie bv – Utrecht/Antwerpen
This edition © Automobile Association Developments Limited 2008
Reprinted July 2008, October 2008

ISBN: 978-0-7495-5669-3

A CIP catalogue record for this book is available from the
British Library

Published by AA Publishing (a trading name of Automobile
Association Developments Limited) whose registered office is
Fanum House, Basingstoke, Hampshire RG21 4EA.
Registered number 1878835

Printed and bound in Italy by Printer Trento S.r.l.

Find out more about AA Publishing and the wide range of
services the AA provides by visiting our web site at
www.aatravelshop.com

A03984

Contents

Introduction 6
Pronunciation table 7

1   Useful lists 9–23

1.1 Today or tomorrow? 10
1.2 Bank holidays 12
1.3 What time is it? 12
1.4 One, two, three ... 14
1.5 The weather 17
1.6 Here, there ... 19
1.7 What does that sign say? 21
1.8 Telephone alphabet 22
1.9 Personal details 23

2   Courtesies 24–32

2.1 Greetings 25
2.2 How to ask a question 26
2.3 How to reply 29
2.4 Thank you 30
2.5 Sorry 30
2.6 What do you think? 31

3   Conversation 33–47

3.1 I beg your pardon? 34
3.2 Introductions 35
3.3 Starting/ending a conversation 39
3.4 Congratulations and condolences 40
3.5 A chat about the weather 40
3.6 Hobbies 41
3.7 Being the host(ess) 41
3.8 Invitations 42
3.9 Paying a compliment 43
3.10 Chatting someone up 44
3.11 Arrangements 46
3.12 Saying goodbye 46

4   Eating out 48–61

4.1 On arrival 49
4.2 Ordering 51
4.3 The bill 55
4.4 Complaints 55
4.5 Paying a compliment 57
4.6 The menu 57
4.7 Alphabetical list of drinks and dishes 58

5   On the road 62–80

5.1 Asking for directions 63
5.2 Customs 64
5.3 Luggage 66
5.4 Traffic signs 70
5.5 The car 71
        The parts of a car 68

5.6 The petrol station 71
5.7 Breakdown and repairs 72
5.8 The bicycle/moped 75
        The parts of a bicycle 76
5.9 Renting a vehicle 78
5.10 Hitchhiking 79

6   Public transport 81–91

6.1 In general 82
6.2 Questions to
        passengers 84
6.3 Tickets 85

6.4 Information 87
6.5 Aeroplanes 89
6.6 Trains 89
6.7 Taxis 90

7   Overnight accommodation 92–103

7.1 General 93
7.2 Camping 94
        Camping equipment 96

7.3 Hotel/B&B/apartment/
        holiday house 99
7.4 Complaints 101
7.5 Departure 103

8   Money matters 104–107

8.1 Banks 105

8.2 Settling the bill 107

9   Post and telephone 108–115

9.1 Post 109

9.2 Telephone 111

10 Shopping 116–128

10.1 Shopping
conversations 117
10.2 Food 120
10.3 Clothing and shoes 121

10.4 Photographs
and video 123
10.5 At the hairdresser's 125

11 At the Tourist Information Centre 129–137

11.1 Places of interest 130
11.2 Going out 133

11.3 Booking tickets 135

12 Sports 138–141

12.1 Sporting questions 139
12.2 By the waterfront 139

12.3 In the snow 141

13 Sickness 142–150

13.1 Call (fetch) the doctor 143
13.2 Patient's ailments 143
13.3 The consultation 144

13.4 Medication and
prescriptions 148
13.5 At the dentist's 149

14 In trouble 151–158

14.1 Asking for help 152
14.2 Loss 153
14.3 Accidents 153

14.4 Theft 155
14.5 Missing person 155
14.6 The police 156

Introduction

● **Welcome to the AA's Pocket Guide Phrase Books series**, covering the most popular European languages and containing everything you'd expect from a comprehensive language series. They're concise, accessible and easy to understand, and you'll find them indispensable on your trip abroad.

Each guide is divided into 14 themed sections and starts with a pronunciation table which gives you the phonetic spelling to all the words and phrases you'll need to know for your trip.

Throughout the book you'll come across coloured boxes with a beside them. These are designed to help you if you can't understand what your listener is saying to you. Hand the book over to them and encourage them to point to the appropriate answer to the question you are asking.

Other coloured boxes in the book - this time without the symbol - give alphabetical listings of themed words with their English translations beside them.

This phrase book covers all subjects you are likely to come across during the course of your visit, from reserving a room for the night to ordering food and drink at a restaurant and what to do if your car breaks down or you lose your traveller's cheques and money. With over 2,000 commonly used words and essential phrases at your fingertips you can rest assured that you will be able to get by in all situations.

Pronunciation table

The pronunciation provided should be read as if it were English, bearing in mind the following main points:

Vowels

Vowels in Spanish are very open

a	is like **a** in **a**mber,	*ah*	as in **casa**	*kahsah*
e	is like **e** in **e**gg,	*eh*	as in **esta**	*ehstah*
i	is like **ee** in s**ee**n,	*ee*	as in **isla**	*eeslah*
o	is like **o** in J**o**hn,	*oh*	as in **hotel**	*ohtehl*
u	is like **oo** in r**oo**m,	*oo*	as in **uno**	*oonoh*
y	is like **ee** in s**ee**n,	*ee*	as in **y**	*ee*

the diphthong **ay** is pronounced as in aisle or eye

as in **hay**   *eye*

Consonants

Consonants are as in English, pronounced less clearly, except

b/v   are pronounced roughly the same

as in **vamos**   *bahmohs*

c   before e and i is soft and is like the **th** in **th**atch

as in **la acera**   *lah ahthehrah*

before a,o and u is hard

as in **cosa**   *kohsah*

cu   before another vowel is pronounced like **cw**

as in **la cuenta**   *lah kwehntah*

g   before e and i is soft and is like the Scottish **ch** in lo**ch**,

as in **la gente**   *lah <u>h</u>ehnteh*

before a, o and u is hard

as in **gato**   *ghahtoh*

gu   before e and i is pronounced as hard **g**

as in **la guía**   *geeah*

before a, o and u is pronounced like **gw**

as in **guapo**   *gwahpoh*

gü	before e and i is pronounced like **gw**		
		as in **lingüística**	*leengweesteekah*
h	is silent		
j	is like the soft **g**	as in **jarra**	*<u>h</u>ahrrah*
ll	is like **ll**i in bi**ll**ion	as in **llave**	*lyahbeh*
ñ	is like **n**i in o**n**ion	as in **año**	*ahnyoh*
r	is rolled as in the Scottish **r**, **rr** is a longer roll		
z	is like **th** in **th**ought	as in **taza**	*tahthah*

The stress normally falls on the last syllable of the word (**hotel**), except that words ending in a vowel (not including **y**) or in n or s (**casa**, **casas**) are stressed on the next to the last syllable. All exceptions are indicated by a written acute accent (**Córdoba**, *kohrdohbah*).

Note: In the south, the soft **c** and the **z** are pronounced **s**. This is also true in Latin America.

1

Useful lists

1.1 Today or tomorrow? 10

1.2 Bank holidays 12

1.3 What time is it? 12

1.4 One, two, three... 14

1.5 The weather 17

1.6 Here, there... 19

1.7 What does that sign say? 21

1.8 Telephone alphabet 22

1.9 Personal details 23

1.1 Today or tomorrow?

What day is it today? __	¿Qué día es hoy? *keh deeah ehs oy?*
Today's Monday _____	Hoy es lunes *oy ehs loonehs*
– Tuesday _____	Hoy es martes *oy ehs mahrtehs*
– Wednesday _____	Hoy es miércoles *oy ehs myehrkohlehs*
– Thursday_____	Hoy es jueves *oy ehs <u>h</u>ooehbehs*
– Friday _____	Hoy es viernes *oy ehs byehrnehs*
– Saturday _____	Hoy es sábado *oy ehs sahbahdoh*
– Sunday _____	Hoy es domingo *oy ehs dohmeengoh*
in January _____	en enero *ehn ehnehroh*
since February _____	desde febrero *dehsdeh fehbrehroh*
in spring_____	en primavera *ehn preemahbehrah*
in summer _____	en verano *ehn behrahnoh*
in autumn_____	en otoño *ehn ohtohnyoh*
in winter _____	en invierno *ehn eenbyehrno*
1997 _____	mil novecientos noventa y siete *meel nohbehthyentohs nohbehntah ee syehteh*
the twentieth century___	el siglo XX (veinte) *ehl seegloh beheenteh*

What's the date today? ¿Qué día es hoy?
keh deeah ehs oy?

Today's the 24th Hoy es 24 (veinticuatro)
oy ehs beheenteekwahtroh

Monday 3 November 1998 lunes 3 (tres) de noviembre de 1998 (mil novecientos noventa y ocho)
loonehs trehs deh nohbyehmbreh deh meel nohbehthyehntohs nohbehntah ee ohchoh

in the morning por la mañana
pohr lah mahnyahnah

in the afternoon por la tarde
pohr lah tahrdeh

in the evening por la noche
pohr lah nohcheh

at night por la noche
pohr lah nohcheh

this morning esta mañana
ehstah mahnyahnah

this afternoon esta tarde
ehstah tahrdeh

this evening esta noche
ehstah nohcheh

tonight esta noche
ehstah nohcheh

last night anoche
ahnohcheh

this week esta semana
ehstah sehmahnah

next month el mes próximo
ehl mehs prohxeemoh

last year el año pasado
ehl ahnyo pahsahdoh

next... el/la... próximo/a
ehl/lah... prohxeemoh/ah

in...days/weeks/ _____	dentro de...días/semanas/meses/años
months/years	*dehntroh deh...*
	deeahs/sehmahnahs/mehsehs/ahnyohs
...weeks ago _____	hace...semanas
	ahthe...sehmahnahs
day off _____	día libre
	deeah leebreh

1.2 Bank holidays

● **The most important** Bank Holidays in Spain are the following:

January 1	New Year's Day (Año Nuevo)
January 6	Epiphany (Epifanía)
March 19	St. Joseph's Day (San José)
March/April	Good Friday (Viernes Santo)
March/April	Easter Monday(Catalonia) (Lunes Santo)
May 1	Labour Day (Día del Trabajo)
May/June	Corpus Christi (Corpus Christi)
July 25	St. James's Day (Santiago)
August 15	Assumption Day (Asunción)
October 12	Columbus Day (Día de las Américas)
November 1	All Saints' Day (Todos los Santos)
December 6	Constitution Day (Día de la Constitución)
December 8	Immaculate Conception (Inmaculada Concepción)
December 25	Christmas (Navidad)

There are also various regional holidays like San Fermín in Pamplona (July 6–13) and the Fallas in Valencia (March 19).

1.3 What time is it?

What time is it? _____	¿Qué hora es?
	keh ohrah ehs?

It's nine o'clock _____	Son las nueve
	sohn lahs nwehbeh
– five past ten _____	Son las diez y cinco
	sohn lahs dyeth ee theenkoh
– a quarter past eleven _	Son las once y cuarto
	sohn lahs ohntheh ee kwahrtoh
– twenty past twelve ___	Son las doce y veinte
	sohn lahs dohthe ee beheenteh
– half past one _____	Es la una y media
	ehs lah oonah ee mehdyah
– twenty–five to three __	Son las tres menos veinticinco
	sohn lahs trehs mehnohs beheenteetheenkoh
– a quarter to four _____	Son las cuatro menos cuarto
	sohn lahs kwahtroh mehnohs kwahrtoh
– ten to five _____	Son las cinco menos diez
	sohn lahs theenkoh mehnohs dyehth
– twelve noon _____	Son las doce del mediodía
	sohn lahs dohtheh dehl mehdyohdeeah
– midnight _____	Son las doce de la noche
	sohn lahs dohtheh deh lah nohcheh
half an hour _____	media hora
	mehdyah ohrah
What time? _____	¿A qué hora?
	ah keh ohrah?
What time can I come _ round?	¿A qué hora puedo pasar?
	ah keh ohrah pwehdoh pahsahr?
At... _____	A las...
	ah lahs...
After... _____	Después de las...
	dehspwehs deh lahs...
Before... _____	Antes de las...
	ahntehs deh lahs...
Between...and... _____	Entre las...y las...
	ehntreh lahs...ee lahs...
From...to... _____	De las...a las...
	deh lahs...ah lahs...

In...minutes _____	Dentro de...minutos
	dehntroh deh...meenootohs
– an hour _____	Dentro de una hora
	dehntroh deh oonah ohrah
– ...hours _____	Dentro de...horas
	dehntroh deh...ohrahs
– a quarter of an hour __	Dentro de un cuarto de hora
	dehntroh deh oon kwahrtoh deh ohrah
– three quarters of _____	Dentro de tres cuartos de hora
an hour	*dehntroh deh trehs kwahrtohs deh ohrah*
early/late _____	muy temprano/tarde
	mwee tehmprahnoh/tahrdeh
on time _____	a tiempo
	ah tyehmpoh
summer opening hours _	horario de verano
	ohrahryoh deh behrahnoh
winter opening hours___	horario de invierno
	ohrahryoh deh eenbyehrnoh

1.4 One, two, three...

0 _____	cero	*thehroh*
1 _____	uno	*oonoh*
2 _____	dos	*dohs*
3 _____	tres	*trehs*
4 _____	cuatro	*kwahtroh*
5 _____	cinco	*theenkoh*
6 _____	seis	*sehees*
7 _____	siete	*syehteh*
8 _____	ocho	*ohchoh*
9 _____	nueve	*nwehbeh*
10 _____	diez	*dyeth*
11 _____	once	*ohntheh*
12 _____	doce	*dohtheh*
13 _____	trece	*trehtheh*

14	_____	catorce	*kahtohrtheh*
15	_____	quince	*keentheh*
16	_____	dieciséis	*dyetheesehees*
17	_____	diecisiete	*dyetheesyehteh*
18	_____	dieciocho	*dyetheeohchoh*
19	_____	diecinueve	*dyetheenwehbe*
20	_____	veinte	*beheenteh*
21	_____	veintiuno	*beheenteeoonoh*
22	_____	veintidós	*beheenteheedohs*
30	_____	treinta	*treheentah*
31	_____	treinta y uno	*treheentah ee oonoh*
32	_____	treinta y dos	*treheentah ee dohs*
40	_____	cuarenta	*kwahrehntah*
50	_____	cincuenta	*theenkwehntah*
60	_____	sesenta	*sehsehntah*
70	_____	setenta	*sehtehntah*
80	_____	ochenta	*ohchehntah*
90	_____	noventa	*nohvehntah*
100	_____	cien	*thyehn*
101	_____	ciento uno	*thyehntoh oonoh*
110	_____	ciento diez	*thyehntoh dyeth*
120	_____	ciento veinte	*thyehntoh beheenteh*
200	_____	doscientos	*dohsthyehntohs*
300	_____	trescientos	*trehsthyehntohs*
400	_____	cuatrocientos	*kwahtrohthyehntohs*
500	_____	quinientos	*keenyehntohs*
600	_____	seiscientos	*seheesthyehntohs*
700	_____	setecientos	*sehtehthyehntohs*
800	_____	ochocientos	*ohchohthyehntohs*
900	_____	novecientos	*nohbehthyentohs*
1000	_____	mil	*meel*
1100	_____	mil cien	*meel thyehn*
2000	_____	dos mil	*dohs meel*
10,000	_____	diez mil	*dyeth meel*
100,000	_____	cien mil	*thyehn meel*
1,000,000	_____	un millón	*oon meelyohn*
1st	_____	primero	*preemehroh*

2nd _____	segundo	*sehgoondoh*
3rd _____	tercero	*tehrthehroh*
4th _____	cuarto	*kwahrtoh*
5th _____	quinto	*keentoh*
6th _____	sexto	*sehxtoh*
7th _____	séptimo	*sehpteemoh*
8th _____	octavo	*ohktahboh*
9th _____	noveno	*nohvehnoh*
10th _____	décimo	*dehtheemoh*
11th _____	undécimo	*oondehtheemoh*
12th _____	duodécimo	*doo-ohdehtheemo*
13th _____	decimotercero	*dehtheemohtehrthehroh*
14th _____	decimocuarto	*dehtheemohkwahrtoh*
15th _____	decimoquinto	*dehtheemohkeentoh*
16th _____	decimosexto	*dehtheemohsehxtoh*
17th _____	decimoséptimo	*dehtheemosehpteemoh*
18th _____	decimoctavo	*dehtheemohktahboh*
19th _____	decimonoveno	*dehtheemonobenoh*
20th _____	vigésimo	*beeheseemoh*
21st _____	vigesimo -primero	*beeheseemohpreemeroh*
22nd _____	vigesimose -gundo	*beeheseemohsegoondoh*
30th _____	trigésimo	*treeheseemoh*
100th _____	centésimo	*thentehseemoh*
1,000th _____	milésimo	*meelehseemoh*
once _____	una vez	*oonah behth*
twice _____	dos veces	*dos behthes*
double _____	el doble	*ehl dohbleh*
triple _____	el triple	*ehl treepleh*
half _____	la mitad	*lah meetath*
a quarter _____	un cuarto	*oon kwartoh*
a third _____	un tercio	*oon terthyoh*
a couple, a few, some __	unos, algunos	*oonohs, algoonohs*
2 + 4 = 6 _____	dos más cuatro, seis	*dohs mahs kwahtroh, sehees*

4 − 2 = 2 _____	cuatro menos dos, dos
	kwahtroh mehnohs dohs, dohs
2 x 4 = 8 _____	dos por cuatro, ocho
	dohs pohr kwahtroh, ohchoh
4 ÷ 2 = 2 _____	cuatro dividido dos, dos
	kwahtroh deebeedeedoh dohs, dohs
odd/even _____	par/impar
	pahr/eempahr
total_____	(en) total
	(ehn) tohtahl
6 x 9 _____	seis por nueve
	sehees pohr nwehbeh

1.5 The weather

Is the weather going to be good/bad?	¿Hará buen/mal tiempo?
	ahrah bwehn/mahl tyehmpoh?
Is it going to get colder/hotter?	¿Hará más frío/calor?
	ahrah mahs freeoh/kahlohr?
What temperature is it going to be?	¿Cuántos grados hará?
	kwahntohs grahdohs ahrah?
Is it going to rain?	¿Va a llover?
	bah ah lyohbehr?
Is there going to be a storm?	¿Tendremos tormenta?
	tehndrehmohs tohrmehntah?
Is it going to snow?	¿Va a nevar?
	bah ah nehbahr?
Is it going to freeze?	¿Va a helar?
	bah ah ehlahr?
Is the thaw setting in?	¿Comenzará el deshielo?
	kohmehnzahrah ehl dehsyeloh
Is it going to be foggy?	¿Habrá niebla?
	ahbrah nyehblah?
Is there going to be a thunderstorm?	¿Habrá tormenta eléctrica?
	ahbrah tohrmehntah ehlehktreekah?

algo nublado/nublado	granizo	ola de calor
light/heavy clouds	hail	heat wave
bochornoso	...grados(bajo/sobre cero)	pesado
stormy	...degrees(above/ below zero)	muggy
bueno		sofocante
fine	helada	scorching hot
caluroso	(black) ice	soleado
hot	húmedo	sunny
chubasco	damp	suave
shower	huracán	mild
cielo cubierto	hurricane	tormenta eléctrica
overcast	llovizna	thunderstorm
desapacible	drizzle	vendaval
bleak	lluvia	gale
despejado	rain	ventoso
clear	lluvioso	windy
escarcha	wet	viento
frost	niebla	wind
fresco	fog	viento leve /moderado/ fuerte
chilly	nieve	light/moderate/ strong wind
frìo	snow	tempestad
cold	nublado cloudy	squall

The weather's _____ changing — Va a cambiar el tiempo
bah ah kahmbyahr ehl tyehmpoh

It's cooling down _____ — Va a refrescar
bah ah rehfrehskahr

What's the weather _____ going to be like today/ tomorrow? — ¿Qué tiempo hará hoy/mañana?
keh tyehmpoh ahrah oy/mahnyahnah?

1.6 Here, there...

See also 5.1 Asking for directions

here/there _____	aquí/allá
	ahkee/ahlyah
somewhere/nowhere ___	en alguna/ninguna parte
	ehn algoonah/neengoonah pahrteh
everywhere _____	en todas partes
	ehn tohdahs pahrtehs
far away/nearby _____	lejos/cerca
	le<u>h</u>os/thehrkah
right/left _____	a la derecha/izquierda
	ah lah dehrehchah/eethkyehrdah
to the right/left of _____	a la derecha/izquierda de
	ah lah dehrehchah/eethkyehrdah deh
straight ahead_____	todo recto
	tohdoh rehktoh
via _____	pasando por
	pahsahndoh pohr
in _____	en
	ehn
on _____	sobre
	sohbreh
under _____	debajo de
	deba<u>h</u>oh deh
against _____	contra
	kohntrah
opposite_____	frente a
	frehnteh ah
next to _____	al lado de
	ahl lahdoh deh
near_____	junto a
	<u>h</u>oontoh ah
in front of _____	delante de
	dehlahnteh deh

in the centre _____	en el medio
	ehn ehl mehdyoh
forward_____	hacia adelante
	ahthyah ahdehlanteh
down_____	(hacia) abajo
	(ahthyah) ahbah<u>h</u>oh
up _____	(hacia) arriba
	(ahthya) ahrreebah
inside _____	(hacia) adentro
	(ahthya) ahdehntroh
outside _____	(hacia) afuera
	(ahthya) ahfwehrah
behind _____	(hacia) atrás
	(ahthya) ahtrahs
at the front_____	delante
	dehlahnteh
at the back _____	detrás
	dehtrahs
in the north _____	en el norte
	ehn ehl nohrteh
to the south_____	hacia el sur
	ahthya ehl soor
from the west _____	del oeste
	dehl ohehsteh
from the east_____	del este
	dehl ehsteh
...of _____	al...de
	ahl...deh

1.7 What does that sign say?

See also 5.4 Traffic signs

abierto/cerrado
open/closed

agua no potable
no drinking water

alta tensión
high voltage

ascensor lift

caballeros
gents/gentlemen

caja pay here

completo full

coto privado
private (property)

cuidado con el perro
beware of the dog

cuidado, escalón
mind the step

entrada
entrance

entrada libre
free admission

escalera stairs

escalera de
incendios
fire escape

escalera mecánica
escalator

freno de emergencia
emergency brake

horario (de apertura)
opening hours

información
information

liquidación (por
cese)
closing-down sale

no funciona
out of order

no tocar
please do not touch

peligro
danger

peligro de incendio
fire hazard

...piso ...floor

primeros auxilios
first aid

prohibido el paso
no entry

prohibido fotografiar
no photographs

prohibido fumar
no smoking

prohibido hacer
fuego
no open fires

prohibido para
animales
no pets allowed

prohibido pisar el
césped
keep off the grass

razón aquí
inquiries

rebajas
clearance

recepción
reception

recién pintado
wet paint

reservado
reserved

saldos
sale

salida
exit

salida de
emergencia/salida
de socorro
emergency exit

se alquila
for hire

se ruega no
molestar
do not disturb

se vende
for sale

señoras
ladies

servicios
toilets

empujar/tirar
push/pull

1.8 Telephone alphabet

a	_ah_	de Antonio	_deh ahntohnyoh_
b	_beh_	de Barcelona	_deh bahr-thehlohnah_
c	_theh_	de Carmen	_deh kahrmehn_
ch	_cheh_	de chocolate	_deh chohkohlahteh_
d	_deh_	de Dolores	_deh dohlohrehs_
e	_eh_	de Enrique	_deh ehnreekeh_
f	_hefeh_	de Francia	_deh frahnthyah_
g	_heh_	de Gerona	_de hehrohnah_
h	_ahcheh_	de historia	_de eestohryah_
I	_ee_	de Inés	_deh eenehs_
j	_hohtah_	de José	_deh hohseh_
k	_kah_	de Kilo	_deh keeloh_
l	_ehleh_	de Lorenzo	_deh lohrehnthoh_
ll	_ehlyeh_	de Llobregat	_deh lyohbrehgaht_
m	_ehmeh_	de Madrid	_deh Mahdreedh_
n	_ehneh_	de Navarra	_deh nahbahrrah_
ñ	_ehnyeh_	de ñoño	_deh nyohnyoh_
o	_oh_	de Oviedo	_deh ohbyedoh_
p	_peh_	de París	_deh pahrees_
q	_koo_	de querido	_deh kehreedoh_
r	_ehrreh_	de Ramón	_deh rahmohn_
s	_ehseh_	de sábado	_deh sahbahdoh_
t	_teh_	de Tarragona	_deh tahrrahgohnah_
u	_oo_	de Ulises	_deh ooleesehs_
v	_oobeh_	de Valencia	_deh bahlehnthyah_
w	_oobehdohbleh_	de Washington	_deh wahsheengtohn_
x	_ehkees_	de Xiquena	_deh heekehnah_
y	_eegryehgah_	griega	_gryehgah_
z	_thehtah_	de Zaragoza	_deh thahrahgohthah_

1.9 Personal details

surname_____	apellidos *ahpehlyeedohs*
christian name(s) _____	nombre *nohmbreh*
initials _____	iniciales
	eeneethyahlehs
address (street/ _____ number)	dirección (calle/número) *deerehkthyohn (kahlyeh/noomehroh)*
	código postal/población
post code/town _____	*cohdeegoh pohstahl/pohblahthyon)*
	sexo (v = varón, m = mujer)
sex (male/female) _____	*sehksoh (v = bahrohn, m = moohehr)*
	nacionalidad
nationality _____	*nahthyohnahleedahd*
	fecha de nacimiento
date of birth_____	*fehchah deh nahtheemyehntoh*
	lugar de nacimiento
place of birth_____	*loogahr deh natheemyehntoh*
	profesión
occupation _____	*profehsyohn*
	casado, casada/soltero, soltera/
married/single/ _____ divorced	divorciado, divorciada *kahsahdoh, kahsahdah/sohltehroh, sohltehrah/deebohrthyahdoh, deebohrthyahdah*
widowed _____	viuda/viudo *byoodah/byoodoh*
(number of) children_____	(número de) hijos *(noomehroh deh) eehohs*
passport/identity _____ card/driving licence/ number, place and date of issue	pasaporte/carnet de identidad/permiso de conducir/número, lugar y fecha de expedición *kahrneh deh eedehnteedahdh (pahsahpohrteh/pehrmeesoh deh kohndootheer) noomehroh, loogahr ee fehchah deh ehkspehdeethyohn*

2 Courtesies

2.1 Greetings 25

2.2 How to ask a question 26

2.3 How to reply 29

2.4 Thank you 30

2.5 Sorry 30

2.6 What do you think? 31

● **Female friends and relatives** kiss on both cheeks in Spain. In shops, etc., you will hear *¡Buenos días!* or just *¡Buenas!*, and expect to be addressed in Basque or Catalan in these provinces. For example you will hear *¡Agur!* instead of *¡Adiós!* in the Basque Country.

2.1 Greetings

Hello, Mr Smith_____	Hola, buenos días
	ohlah, bwehnohs deeahs
Hello, Peter _____	Hola, Pedro
	ohlah, pehdroh
Hi, Helen _____	Qué hay, Elena
	keh ay, ehlehnah
Good morning, madam_	Buenos días, señora (before 2pm)
	bwehnohs deeahs, sehnyohrah
Good afternoon, sir ____	Buenas tardes, señor (after 2pm)
	bwehnahs tahrdehs, sehnyohr
Good evening _____	Buenas tardes (before 9pm), buenas noches (after 9pm)
	bwehnahs tahrdehs, bwehnahs nohchehs
How are you? _____	¿Qué tal?
	keh tahl?
Fine, thank you, and ___ you?	Muy bien, ¿y usted?
	mwee byehn, ee oostehdh?
Very well_____	Estupendo
	ehstoopehndoh
Not very well_____	Regular
	rehgoolahr
Not too bad_____	Tirando
	teerando
I'd better be going ____	Bueno, me voy
	bwehnoh, meh boy
I have to be going._____ Someone's waiting for me	Tengo que irme. Me están esperando *tehngoh keh eermeh, meh ehstahn ehspehrahndoh*

25

Bye!_____	¡Adiós!
	ahdyohs!
Goodbye _____	Hasta luego
	ahstah lwehgoh
See you soon _____	Hasta pronto
	ahstah prohntoh
See you later_____	Hasta luego
	ahstah lwehgoh
See you in a little while _	Hasta ahora
	ahstah ahohrah
Sleep well _____	Que descanse
	keh dehskahnseh
Good night _____	Buenas noches
	bwehnahs nohchehs
All the best _____	Que le vaya bien
	keh leh bahyah byehn
Have fun _____	Que se divierta, que lo pase bien
	keh seh deebyehrtah, keh loh pahseh byehn
Good luck _____	Mucha suerte
	moochah swehrteh
Have a nice holiday ____	Felices vacaciones
	fehleethehs bahkahthyohnehs
Have a good trip _____	Buen viaje
	bwehn byahheh
Thank you, you too ____	Gracias, igualmente
	grahthyahs, eegwahlmehnteh
Say hello to...for me ___	Recuerdos a...
	rehkwehrdohs ah...

2.2 How to ask a question

Who? _____	¿Quién?
	kyehn?
Who's that? _____	¿Quién es?
	kyehn ehs?

What? _____	¿Qué?
	keh?
What's there to _____ see here?	¿Qué se puede visitar aquí?
	keh seh pwehdeh beeseetahr ahkee?
What kind of hotel _____ is that?	¿Qué clase de hotel es?
	keh klahseh deh ohtehl ehs?
Where? _____	¿Dónde?
	dohndeh?
Where's the toilet? _____	¿Dónde están los servicios?
	dohndeh ehstahn lohs sehrbeethyohs?
Where are you going? __	¿A dónde va?
	ahdohndeh bah?
Where are you from? ___	¿De dónde es usted?
	deh dohndeh ehs oostehdh?
How? _____	¿Cómo?
	kohmoh?
How far is that? _____	¿A qué distancia queda?
	ah keh deestahnthyah kehdah?
How long does it take?_	¿Cuánto dura?
	kwahntoh doorah?
How long is the trip? ___	¿Cuánto dura el viaje?
	kwahntoh doorah ehl byahheh?
How much?_____	¿Cuánto?
	kwahntoh?
How much is this? _____	¿Cuánto vale?
	kwahntoh bahleh?
What time is it? _____	¿Qué hora es?
	keh ohrah ehs?
Which? _____	¿Cuál? ¿Cuáles?
	kwahl? kwahlehs?
Which glass is mine? __	¿Cuál es mi copa?
	kwahl ehs mee kohpah?
When? _____	¿Cuándo?
	kwahndoh?
When are you leaving? _	¿Cuándo sale?
	kwahndoh sahleh?

English	Spanish / Pronunciation
Why? _____	¿Por qué?
	pohr keh?
Could you...me? _____	¿Podría...?
	pohdreeah...?
Could you help me, ____ please?	¿Podría ayudarme?
	pohdreeah ahyoodahrmeh?
Could you point that ___ out to me?	¿Me lo podría indicar?
	meh loh pohdreeah eendeekahr?
Could you come_____ with me, please?	¿Le importaría acompañarme?
	leh eempohrtahreeah ahkohmpahnyahrmeh?
Could you..._____	¿Quiere...?/¿Podría...?
	kyehreh...?/pohdreeah...?
Could you reserve some tickets for me, please?	¿Me podría reservar entradas?
	meh pohdreeah rehsehrbahr ehntrahdahs?
Do you know...? _____	¿Sabe...?
	sahbeh...?
Do you know another __ hotel, please?	¿Sabría indicarme otro hotel?
	sahbreeah eendeekahrmeh ohtroh ohtehl?
Do you know _____ whether...?	¿Tiene...?
	tyehneh...?
Do you have a...?_____	¿Me podría dar un(a)...?
	meh pohdreeah dahr oon(ah)...?
Do you have a _____ vegetarian dish, please?	¿Tendría un plato sin carne?
	tehndreeah oon plahtoh seen kahrneh?
I'd like... _____	Quisiera...
	keesyehrah...
I'd like a kilo of apples, _ please.	Quisiera un kilo de manzanas
	keesyehrah oon keeloh deh mahnthahnahs
Can I...? _____	¿Puedo...?/¿Se puede...?
	pwehdoh...?/seh pwehdeh?
Can I take this? _____	¿Podría llevármelo?
	pohdreeah lyehbahrmehloh?
Can I smoke here?_____	¿Se puede fumar aquí?
	seh pwehdeh foomahr ahkee?
Could I ask you _____ something?	¿Puedo hacerle una pregunta?
	pwehdoh ahthehrleh oonah prehgoontah?

2.3 How to reply

Yes, of course _____ Sí, claro
see, klahroh

No, I'm sorry _____ No, lo siento
noh, loh syehntoh

Yes, what can I do _____ Sí. ¿En qué puedo servirle?
for you? *see, ehn keh pwehdoh sehrbeerleh?*

Just a moment, please _ Un momento, por favor
oon mohmehntoh, pohr fahbohr

No, I don't have _____ No, ahora no tengo tiempo
time now *noh, aohrah noh tehngoh tyehmpoh*

No, that's impossible___ No, eso es imposible
noh, ehsoh ehs eempohseebleh

I think so _____ Creo que sí
krehoh keh see

I agree _____ Yo también lo creo
yoh tahmbyehn loh krehoh

I hope so too_____ Yo también lo espero
yoh tahmbyehn loh ehspehroh

No, not at all _____ No, de ninguna manera
noh, deh neengoonah mahnehrah

No, no-one _____ No, nadie
noh, nahdyeh

No, nothing _____ No, nada
noh, nahdah

That's (not) right _____ (No) es cierto
(noh) ehs thyehrtoh

I (don't) agree _____ (No) estoy de acuerdo con usted
*(noh) ehstoy deh ahkwehrdoh kohn
oostehdh*

All right_____ Está bien
ehstah byehn

Okay _____ Vale
bahleh

Perhaps _____	Quizá
	keethah
I don't know _____	No lo sé
	noh loh seh

2.4 Thank you

Thank you _____	Gracias
	grahthyahs
You're welcome _____	De nada
	deh nahdah
Thank you very much __	Muchísimas gracias
	moocheeseemahs grahthyahs
Very kind of you _____	Muy amable (de su parte)
	mwee ahmahbleh (deh soo pahrteh)
I enjoyed it very much__	Ha sido un verdadero placer
	ah seedoh oon behrdahdehroh plahthehr
Thank you for your_____	Gracias por la molestia
trouble	*grahthyahs pohr lah mohlehstyah*
You shouldn't have ____	No se hubiera molestado
	noh seh oobyehrah mohlehstahdoh
That's all right _____	No se preocupe
	noh seh prehohkoopeh

2.5 Sorry

Excuse me_____	Perdone
	pehrdohneh
Sorry! _____	¡Perdone!
	pehrdohneh!
I'm sorry, I didn't _____	Perdone, no sabía que...
know...	*pehrdohneh, noh sahbeeah keh...*
I do apologise_____	Perdone
	pehrdohneh

I'm sorry _____	Lo siento
	loh syehntoh
I didn't do it on _____ purpose, it was an accident	No ha sido a propósito; ha sido sin querer
	noh ah seedoh ah prohpohseetoh; ah seedoh seen kehrehr
That's all right _____	No importa
	noh eempohrtah
Never mind _____	Déjelo
	dehhehloh
It could've happened __ to anyone	Le puede pasar a cualquiera
	leh pwehdeh pahsahr ah kwahlkyehrah

2.6 What do you think?

Which do you prefer? __	¿Qué prefiere?
	keh prehfyehreh?
What do you think? ____	¿Qué te parece?
	keh teh pahrehtheh?
Don't you like dancing?	¿No te gusta bailar?
	noh teh goostah bahylahr?
I don't mind_____	Me da igual
	meh dah eegwahl
Well done! _____	¡Muy bien!
	mwee byehn!
Not bad!_____	¡No está mal!
	noh ehstah mahl!
Great! _____	¡Excelente!
	ehxthehlehnteh!
Wonderful! _____	¡Qué delicia!
	keh dehleethyah!
It's really nice here! ____	¡Qué bien se está aquí!
	keh byehn seh ehstah ahkee!
How nice!_____	¡Qué mono/bonito!
	keh mohnoh/bohneetoh!

How nice for you!_____	¡Cuánto me alegro por usted!
	kwahntoh meh ahlehgroh pohr oostehdh!
I'm (not) very happy_____ with...	(No) estoy muy contento con...
	(noh) ehstoy mwee kohntehntoh kohn...
I'm glad..._____	Me alegro de que...
	meh ahlehgroh deh keh...
I'm having a great time _	Me lo estoy pasando muy bien
	meh loh ehstoy pahsahndoh mwee byehn
I'm looking forward to it	Me hace ilusión
	meh ahtheh eeloosyohn
I hope it'll work out _____	Espero que salga bien
	ehspehroh keh sahlgah byehn
That's ridiculous! _____	¡Qué ridículo!
	keh reedeekooloh!
That's terrible!_____	¡Qué horrible!
	keh ohrreebleh!
What a pity!_____	¡Qué lástima!
	keh lahsteemah!
That's filthy!_____	¡Qué asco!
	keh ahskoh!
What a load of _____ rubbish!	¡Qué tontería!
	keh tohntehreeah!
I don't like... _____	No me gusta...
	noh meh goostah...
I'm bored to death_____	Me aburro como una ostra
	meh ahboorroh kohmoh oonah ohstrah
I've had enough _____	Estoy harto(a)
	ehstoy ahrtoh(ah)
This is no good_____	No puede ser
	noh pwehdeh sehr
I was expecting _____ something completely different	Yo me había esperado otra cosa
	yoh meh ahbeeah ehspehrahdoh ohtrah kohsah

3 Conversation

3.1 I beg your pardon? 34

3.2 Introductions 35

3.3 Starting/ending a conversation 39

3.4 Congratulations and condolences 40

3.5 A chat about the weather 40

3.6 Hobbies 41

3.7 Being the host(ess) 41

3.8 Invitations 42

3.9 Paying a compliment 43

3.10 Chatting someone up 44

3.11 Arrangements 46

3.12 Saying goodbye 46

3.1 I beg your pardon?

I don't speak any/ _____ I speak a little...	No hablo/hablo un poco de... *noh ahbloh/ahbloh oon pohkoh deh...*
I'm English_____	Soy inglés/inglesa *soy eenglehs/eenglehsah*
I'm Scottish _____	Soy escocés/escocesa *soy ehskohthehs/ehskothehsah*
I'm Irish _____	Soy irlandés/irlandesa *soy eerlahndehs/eerlahndehsah*
I'm Welsh_____	soy galés/galesa *soy gahlehs/gahlehsah*
Do you speak _____ English/French/ German?	¿Habla inglés/francés/alemán? *ahblah eenglehs/frahnthehs/ahlehmahn?*
Is there anyone who ___ speaks...?	¿Hay alguien que hable...? *ay ahlgyehn ahkee keh ahbleh...?*
I beg your pardon? ____	¿Cómo dice? *kohmoh deeteh?*
I (don't) understand ____	(No) comprendo *(noh) kohmprehndoh*
Do you understand ____ me?	¿Me entiende? *meh ehntyehndeh?*
Could you repeat that, _ please?	¿Le importa repetirlo? *leh eempohrtah rehpehteerloh?*
Could you speak more _ slowly, please?	¿Podría hablar más despacio? *pohdreeah ahblahr mahs dehspahthyo?*
What does that (word)__ mean?	¿Qué significa esto/esta palabra? *keh seegneefeekah ehstoh/ehstah pahlahbrah?*
Is that similar to/the____ same as...?	¿Es (más o menos) lo mismo que...? *ehs mahs oh mehnohs loh meesmoh keh...?*
Could you write that ___ down for me, please?	¿Podría escribírmelo? *pohdreeah eskreebeermehloh?*

Could you spell that ___ ¿Podría deletreármelo?
 for me, please?   *pohdreeah dehlehtrehahrmehloh?*

(See 1.8 Telephone alphabet)

Could you point that ___ ¿Me lo podría señalar en esta guía?
 out in this phrase   *meh loh pohdreeah sehnyahlahr ehn*
 book, please?   *ehstah gheeah?*
One moment, please, __ Espere que lo busco en la guía
 I have to look it up   *ehspehreh keh loh booskoh ehn*
             lah gheeah
I can't find the_____ No puedo encontrar la palabra/la frase
 word/the sentence   *noh pwehdoh ehnkohntrahr lah*
             pahlahbrah/lah frahseh
How do you say _____ ¿Cómo se dice eso en...?
 that in...?   *kohmoh seh deetheh ehstoh ehn...?*
How do you pronounce ¿Cómo se pronuncia?
 that?   *kohmoh seh prohnoonthyah?*

3.2 Introductions

May I introduce myself? Permítame presentarme
             pehrmeetahmeh prehsehntahrmeh
My name's... _____ Me llamo...
             meh lyahmoh...
I'm... _____ Soy...
             soy...
What's your name? ____ ¿Cómo se llama?
             kohmoh seh lyahmah?
May I introduce...?_____ Permítame presentarle a...
             pehrmeetahmeh prehsehntahrleh ah...
This is my wife/ _____ Esta es mi mujer/mi hija/mi madre/mi
 daughter/mother/   amiga
 girlfriend   *ehstah ehs mee moohehr/mee eehah*
             /mee mahdreh/mee ahmeegah

– my husband/son/ ____ father/boyfriend.	Este es mi marido/mi hijo/mi padre/mi amigo
	ehsteh ehs mee mahreedoh/mee ee<u>h</u>oh/mee pahdreh/mee ahmeegoh
How do you do_____	Hola, mucho gusto
	ohlah, moochoh goostoh
Pleased to meet you ___	Encantado(a) (de conocerle)
	ehnkahntahdoh(ah) (deh kohnohthehrleh)
Where are you from?___	¿De dónde es usted?
	deh dohndeh ehs oostehdh?
I'm from _____ England/Scotland/ Ireland/Wales	Soy inglés/esa escocés/esa irlandés/esa galés/esa
	soy eenglehs/ehsah ehskohthehs/ehsah eerlahndehs/ehsah gahlehs/ ehsah
What city do you live___ in?	¿En qué ciudad vive?
	ehn keh thyoodahdh beebeh?
In..., It's near... _____	En...Eso está cerca de...
	ehn...ehsoh ehstah thehrkah deh...
Have you been here ___ long?	¿Hace mucho que está aquí?
	ahtheh moochoh keh ehstah ahkee?
A few days_____	Unos días
	oonohs deeahs
How long are you_____ staying here?	¿Cuánto tiempo piensa quedarse?
	kwahntoh tyehmpoh pyehnsah kehdahrseh?
We're (probably) _____ leaving tomorrow/ in two weeks	Nos iremos (probablemente) mañana/dentro de dos semanas
	nohs eerehmohs (prohbahblehmehnteh) mahnyahnah/dehntroh deh dohs sehmahnahs
Where are you _____ staying?	¿Dónde se aloja?
	dohndeh seh ahloh<u>h</u>ah?
In a hotel/an apartment_	En un hotel/apartamento
	ehn oon ohtehl/ahpahrtahmehntoh
On a camp site_____	En un camping
	ehn oon kahmpeen

With friends/relatives ___	En casa de amigos/parientes	
	ehn kahsah deh ahmeegohs/pahryehntehs	
Are you here on your ___ own/with your family?	¿Ha venido solo(a)/con su familia?	
	ah behneedoh sohloh(ah)/kohn soo fahmeelyah?	
I'm on my own _____	He venido solo(a)	
	eh behneedoh sohloh(ah)	
I'm with my _____ partner/wife/husband	con mi pareja/mujer/marido	
	kohn mee pahreh<u>hh</u>ah/moo<u>h</u>ehr/mahreedoh	
– with my family _____	con mi familia	
	kohn mee fahmeelyah	
– with relatives _____	con unos parientes	
	kohn oonohs pahryehntehs	
– with a friend/friends __	con un amigo/una amiga/unos amigos	
	kohn oon ahmeegoh/oonah ahmeegah/oonohs ahmeegohs	
Are you married? _____	¿Está casado/casada?	
	ehstah kahsahdoh/kahsahdah?	
Do you have a steady __ boyfriend/girlfriend?	¿Tienes novio/novia?	
	tyehnehs nohbyoh/nohbyah?	
That's none of your ____ business	No es asunto suyo	
	noh ehs ahsoontoh sooyoh	
I'm married _____	Soy casado	
	soy kahsahdoh	
– single_____	Soy soltero	
	soy sohltehroh	
– separated _____	Estoy separado	
	ehstoy sehpahrahdoh	
– divorced _____	Estoy divorciado	
	ehstoy deebohrthyahdoh	
– a widow/widower ____	Soy viuda/viudo	
	soy byoodah/byoodoh	
I live alone/with_____ someone	Vivo solo(a)/con otra persona	
	beeboh sohloh(ah)/kohn ohtrah pehrsohnah	
Do you have any _____ children/grandchildren?	¿Tiene hijos/nietos?	
	tyehneh ee<u>h</u>ohs/nyehtohs?	

How old are you? _____	¿Cuántos años tiene?
	kwahntohs ahnyohs tyehneh?
How old is she/he? ____	¿Cuántos años tiene?
	kwahntohs ahnyohs tyehneh?
I'm... _____	Tengo...años
	tehngoh...ahnyohs
She's/he's..._____	Tiene...años
	tyehneh...ahnyohs
What do you do for a __ living?	¿En qué trabaja?
	ehn keh trahbahhah?
I work in an office_____	Trabajo en una oficina
	trahbahhoh ehn oonah ohfeetheenah
I'm a student/ _____ I'm at school	Estudio
	ehstoodyoh
I'm unemployed _____	Estoy en paro
	ehstoy ehn pahroh
I'm retired _____	Soy jubilado
	soy hoobeelahdoh
I'm on a disability_____ pension	Tengo una pensión de invalidez
	tehngoh oonah pehnsyohn deh eenbahleedeth
I'm a housewife _____	Soy ama de casa
	soy ahmah deh kahsah
Do you like your job? __	¿Le gusta su trabajo?
	leh goostah soo trahbahhoh?
Most of the time_____	A veces sí, a veces no
	ah behthehs see, ah behthehs noh
I usually do, but I _____ prefer holidays	Por lo general sí, pero prefiero las vacaciones
	pohr loh hehnehrahl see, pehroh prehfyehroh lahs bahkahthyohnehs

3.3 Starting/ending a conversation

Could I ask you _____ something?	¿Podría preguntarle una cosa? _pohdreeah prehgoontahrleh oonah kohsah?_
Excuse me_____	Perdone _pehrdohneh_
Excuse me, could you___ help me?	¿Podría ayudarme? _pohdreeah ahyoodahrmeh?_
Yes, what's the problem? _____	Sí, ¿qué pasa? _see, keh pahsah?_
What can I do for you? _	¿En qué puedo servirle? _ehn keh pwehdoh sehrbeerleh?_
Sorry, I don't have time_ now	Lo siento, ahora no tengo tiempo _loh syehntoh, ahohrah noh tehngoh tyehmpoh_
Do you have a light? ___	¿Tiene fuego? _tyehneh fwehgoh?_
May I join you? _____	¿Le importa que me siente? _leh eempohrtah keh meh syehnteh?_
Could you take a _____ picture of me/us? Press this button.	¿Podría sacarme/sacarnos una foto? Hay que apretar este botón _pohdreeah sahkahrmeh/sahkahrnohs oonah fohtoh? ay keh ahprehtahr ehsteh bohtohn_
Leave me alone _____	Déjeme en paz _deh<u>h</u>ehmeh ehn pahth_
Get lost _____	Váyase al diablo _bahyahseh ahl deeahbloh_
Go away or I'll scream _	Como no se vaya, grito _kohmoh noh seh bahyah, greetoh_

3.4 Congratulations and condolences

Happy birthday/many ___ happy returns	Feliz cumpleaños/felicidades *fehleeth koomplehahnyohs/fehleetheedahdehs*
Please accept my _____ condolences.	Le acompaño en el sentimiento *leh ahkohmpahnyoh ehn ehl sehnteemyehntoh*
I'm very sorry for you ___	¡Cuánto lo siento por usted! *kwahntoh loh syehntoh pohr oostehdh!*

3.5 A chat about the weather

See also 1.5 The weather

It's so hot/cold today! ___	¡Qué calor/frío hace hoy! *keh kahlohr/freeoh ahtheh oy!*
Nice weather, isn't it? ___	¡Qué buen tiempo hace! ¿Verdad? *keh bwehn tyehmpoh ahtheh! behrdah?*
What a wind/storm! _____	¡Vaya viento/tormenta! *bahyah byehntoh/tohrmentah!*
All that rain/snow! _____	¡Cómo llueve/nieva! *kohmoh lywehbeh/nyehbah!*
All that fog! _____	¡Cuánta niebla! *kwahntah nyehblah!*
Has the weather been ___ like this for long here?	¿Hace mucho que hace este tiempo? *ahtheh moochoh keh ahtheh ehsteh tyehmpoh?*
Is it always this _____ hot/cold here?	¿Aquí siempre hace tanto calor/frío? *ahkee syehmpreh ahtheh tahntoh kahlohr/freeoh?*
Is it always this _____ dry/wet here?	¿Aquí siempre hace un tiempo tan seco/lluvioso? *ahkee syehmpreh ahtheh oon tyehmpoh tahn sehkoh/lyoobyohsoh?*

3.6 Hobbies

Do you have any _____ hobbies?	¿Tiene algún hobby? *tyehneh algoon hohbee?*
I like painting/ _____ reading/photography/ DIY	Me gusta pintar/leer/la fotografía/el bricolaje *meh goostah peentahr/lehehr/lah fohtohgrahfeeah/ehl breekohlahheh*
I like music _____	Me gusta la música *meh goostah lah mooseekah*
I like playing the _____ guitar/piano	Me gusta tocar la guitarra/el piano *meh goostah tohkahr lah gueetahrrah/ehl pyahnoh*
I like going to the _____ movies	Me gusta ir al cine *meh goostah eer ahl theeneh*
I like travelling/ _____ sport/fishing/walking	Me gusta viajar/hacer deporte/pescar/salir a caminar *meh goostah byahhahr/ahthehr dehpohrteh/pehskahr/sahleer ah kahmeenahr*

3.7 Being the host(ess)

See also 4 Eating out

Can I offer you a _____ drink?	¿Le gustaría algo de beber? *leh goostahreeah ahlgoh deh behbehr?*
What would you like ___ to drink?	¿Qué quieres beber? *keh kyehrehs behbehr?*
Something non- _____ alcoholic, please.	Algo sin alcohol *ahlgoh seen ahlkohl*

Would you like a _____ cigarette/cigar/to roll your own?	¿Quiere un cigarrillo/un puro/liar un cigarrillo? *kyehreh oon theegahrreelyoh/oon pooroh/leeahr oon theegahrreelyoh?*
I don't smoke _____	No fumo *noh foomoh*

3.8 Invitations

Are you doing anything _ tonight?	¿Tiene algo que hacer esta noche? *tyehneh ahlgoh keh ahthehr ehstah nohcheh?*
Do you have any plans _ for today/this afternoon/tonight?	¿Ya tiene planes para hoy/ esta tarde/esta noche? *yah tyehneh plahnehs pahrah oy/ehstah tahrdeh/ehstah nohcheh?*
Would you like to go ___ out with me?	¿Le(te) apetece salir conmigo? *leh(teh) ahpehtehtheh sahleer kohnmeegoh?*
Would you like to go ___ dancing with me?	¿Le(te) apetece ir a bailar conmigo? *leh(teh) ahpehtehtheh eer ah baylahr kohnmeegoh?*
Would you like to have _ lunch/dinner with me?	¿Le(te) apetece comer/cenar conmigo? *leh(teh) ahpehtehtheh kohmehr/thenahr kohnmeegoh?*
Would you like to come to the beach with me?	¿Le(te) apetece ir a la playa conmigo? *leh(teh) ahpehtehtheh eer ah lah plahyah kohnmeegoh?*
Would you like to comeinto town with us?	¿Le apetece ir a la ciudad con nosotros? *leh ahpehtehtheh eer ah lah thyoodahdh kohn nohsohtrohs?*
Would you like to _____ come and see some friends with us?	¿Le apetece ir a casa de unos amigos con nosotros? *leh ahpehtehtheh eer ah kahsah deh oonohs ahmeegohs kohn nohsohtrohs?*

Shall we dance? _____	¿Bailamos?
	baylahmohs?
– sit at the bar? _____	¿Vienes a sentarte conmigo en la barra?
	byehnehs ah sehntahrteh kohnmeegoh ehn lah bahrrah?
– get something to _____ drink?	¿Vamos a beber algo?
	bahmohs ah behbehr ahlgoh?
– go for a walk/drive? __	¿Vamos a dar una vuelta?
	bahmohs ah dahr oonah bwehltah?
Yes, all right_____	Sí, vamos
	see, bahmohs
Good idea _____	Buena idea
	bwehnah eedehah
No (thank you) _____	No (gracias)
	noh (grahthyahs)
Maybe later _____	Quizá más tarde
	keethah mahs tahrdeh
I don't feel like it_____	No me apetece
	noh meh ahpehtehtheh
I don't have time _____	No tengo tiempo
	noh tehngoh tyehmpoh
I already have a date ___	Ya tengo otro compromiso
	yah tehngoh ohtroh kohmprohmeesoh
I'm not very good at ___ dancing/volleyball/ swimming	No sé bailar/jugar al vóleibol/nadar
	noh seh baylahr/<u>h</u>oogahr ahl vohleheebohl/nahdahr

3.9 Paying a compliment

You look wonderful!____	¡Qué guapo/guapa está(estás)!
	keh wahpoh/wahpah ehstah(ehstahs)!
I like your car! _____	¡Qué bonito coche!
	keh bohneetoh kohcheh!
I like your ski outfit! ____	¡Qué bonito traje de esquiar!
	keh bohneetoh trah<u>h</u>eh deh ehskeeahr!

You're a nice boy/girl___	Eres muy bueno/buena
	ehrehs mwee bwehnoh/bwehnah
What a sweet child! ____	¡Qué niño tan majo/niña tan maja!
	keh neenyoh tahn mahhoh/neenyah tahn mahhah!
You're a wonderful_____ dancer!	Bailas muy bien
	bahylahs mwee byehn
You're a wonderful_____ cook!	Cocinas muy bien
	kohtheenahs mwee byehn
You're a terrific soccer _ player!	Juegas muy bien al fútbol
	hwehgahs mwee byehn ahl footbohl

3.10 Chatting someone up

I like being with you____	Me gusta estar contigo
	meh goostah ehstahr kohnteegoh
I've missed you so____ much	Te he echado mucho de menos
	teh eh ehchahdoh moochoh deh mehnohs
I dreamt about you ____	He soñado contigo
	eh sohnyahdoh kohnteegoh
I think about you _____ all day	Pienso todo el día en ti
	pyehnsoh tohdoh ehl deeah ehn tee
You have such a sweet _ smile	Tienes una sonrisa muy bonita
	tyehnehs oonah sohnreesah mwee bohneetah
You have such _____ beautiful eyes	Tienes unos ojos muy bonitos
	tyehnehs oonohs ohhohs mwee bohneetohs
I'm in love with you ____	Estoy enamorado/enamorada de ti
	ehstoy ehnahmohrahdoh/ehnahmohrahdah deh tee
I'm in love with you too_	Yo también de ti
	yoh tahmbyehn deh tee
I love you _____	Te quiero
	teh kyehroh

I love you too _____	Yo también a ti
	yoh tahmbyehn ah tee
I don't feel as strongly__ about you	Yo no siento lo mismo por ti
	yoh noh syehntoh loh meesmoh pohr tee
I already have a _____ boyfriend/girlfriend	Ya tengo pareja
	yah tehngoh pahreh<u>hh</u>ah
I'm not ready for that___	Yo no estoy preparado(a)
	yoh noh ehstoy prehpahrahdoh/ah
This is going too fast___ for me	Vamos demasiado rápido
	bahmohs dehmahsyahdoh rahpeedoh
Take your hands _____ off me	No me toque(s)
	noh meh tohkeh(s)
Okay, no problem_____	Vale, no importa
	bahleh, noh eempohrtah
Will you stay with me __ tonight?	¿Te quedas a dormir?
	teh kehdahs ah dohrmeer?
I'd like to go to bed ____ with you	Me gustaría acostarme contigo
	meh goostahreeah ahkohstahrmeh kohnteegoh
Only if we use a _____ condom	Sólo si usamos condón
	sohloh see oosahmohs kohndohn
We have to be careful __ about AIDS	Hay que tener cuidado por lo del Sida
	ay keh tehnehr kweedahdoh pohr loh dehl seedah
That's what they_____ all say	Eso es lo que dicen todos
	ehsoh ehs loh keh deetehhn tohdohs
We shouldn't take any__ risks	Más vale no arriesgarse
	mahs bahleh noh ahrryehsgahrseh
Do you have a _____ condom?	¿Llevas condones?
	lyehbahs kohndohnehs?
No? In that case we ___ won't do it	¿No? Pues entonces no
	noh? pwehs ehntohnthehs noh

3.11 Arrangements

When will I see _____ you again?	¿Cuándo te veo? _kwahndoh teh behoh?_
Are you free over the____ weekend?	¿Tiene tiempo este fin de semana? _tyehneh tyehmpoh ehsteh feen deh sehmahnah?_
What shall we _____ arrange?	¿Cómo quedamos? _kohmoh kehdahmohs?_
Where shall we meet?__	¿Dónde nos encontramos? _dohndeh nohs ehnkohntrahmohs?_
Will you pick _____ me/us up?	¿Me/nos pasa a buscar? _meh/nohs pahsah ah booskahr?_
Shall I pick you up? ____	¿Lo/la paso a buscar? _loh/lah pahsoh ah booskahr?_
I have to be home by..._	Tengo que estar en casa a las... _tehngoh keh ehstahr ehn kahsah ah lahs..._
I don't want to see____ you anymore	No quiero volver a verlo/verla _noh kyehroh bohlbehr ah behrloh/behrlah_

3.12 Saying goodbye

Can I take you home?__	¿Lo/la acompaño a su casa? _loh/lah ahkohmpahnyoh ah soo kahsah?_
Can I write/call you? ___	¿Puedo escribirle/llamarlo/llamarla por teléfono? _pwehdoh ehskreebeerleh /lyahmahrloh/ lyahmahrlah pohr tehlehfohnoh?_
Will you write/call me? _	¿Me escribirá/llamará por teléfono? _meh ehskreebeerah/lyahmahrah pohr tehlehfohnoh?_
Can I have your _____ address/phone number?	¿Me da su dirección/número de teléfono? _meh dah soo deerehkthyohn/noomehroh deh tehlehfohnoh?_

Thanks for everything	Gracias por todo *grahthyahs pohr tohdoh*
It was very nice	Lo hemos pasado muy bien *loh ehmohs pahsahdoh mwee byehn*
Say hello to...	Recuerdos a... *rehkwehrdohs ah...*
All the best	Te deseo lo mejor *teh dehsehoh loh meh<u>h</u>ohr*
Good luck	Que te vaya bien *keh teh bahyah byehn*
When will you be back?	¿Cuándo vuelves? *kwahndoh bwehlbehs?*
I'll be waiting for you	Te esperaré *teh ehspehrahreh.*
I'd like to see you again	Me gustaría volver a verte *meh goostahreeah bohlbehr ah behrteh*
I hope we meet again soon	Espero que nos volvamos a ver pronto *ehspehroh keh nohs bohlbahmohs ah behr prohntoh*
This is our address. If you're ever in the UK	Esta es nuestra dirección. Si alguna vez pasa por el Reino Unido... *ehstah ehs nwehstrah deerehkthyohn. see ahlgoonah behth pahsah pohr ehl reheenoh ooneedoh...*
You'd be more than welcome	Está cordialmente invitado *ehstah kohrdyahlmehnteh eenbeetahdoh*

4

Eating out

4.1 On arrival 49

4.2 Ordering 51

4.3 The bill 55

4.4 Complaints 55

4.5 Paying a compliment 57

4.6 The menu 57

4.7 Alphabetical list of drinks and dishes 58

● **In Spain** people usually have three meals:

1 *El desayuno* (breakfast) approximately between 7 and 10am. Breakfast is light and consists of *café con leche* (white coffee), a croissant or *suizo* (light sugary bun) or *tostadas* (toast).

2 *El almuerzo* (lunch) approx. between 2 and 4pm, though hotels usually serve at standard times. Lunch always includes a hot dish and is the most important meal of the day. Office workers and schoolchildren still lunch at home. It usually consists of four courses:

– starter (which can be a plate of greens)
– main course
– dessert
– fruit

3 *La cena* (dinner) between 9 and 11pm, 8pm in most hotels. Dinner is usually a light, hot meal, taken with the family.

At around 6 or 7pm, a snack (*la merienda*) is often served, consisting frequently of sandwiches with *chorizo* or *jamón serrano* and *pastas* (biscuits) or small cakes.

Pinchos and *tapas* are often taken at bars with an apéritif, either in the late morning or the evening.

4.1 On arrival

I'd like to book a table for seven o'clock, please	¿Podría reservar una mesa para las siete?
	pohdreeah rehsehrbahr oonah mehsah pahrah lahs syehteh?
I'd like a table for two, please	Quisiera una mesa para dos personas
	keesyehrah oonah mehsah pahrah dohs pehrsohnahs
We've/we haven't booked	(No) hemos reservado
	(noh) ehmohs rehsehrbahdoh
Is the restaurant open yet?	¿Ya está abierto el restaurante?
	yah ehstah ahbyehrtoh ehl rehstahoorahnteh?

¿Ha reservado mesa?	Do you have a reservation?
¿A nombre de quién?	What name, please?
Por aquí, por favor.	This way, please
Esta mesa está reservada	This table is reserved
En quince minutos quedará libre una mesa	We'll have a table free in fifteen minutes.
¿Le importaría esperar (en la barra)?	Would you like to wait (at the bar)?

What time does the _____
restaurant open/close?
¿A qué hora abre/cierra el restaurante?
ah keh ohrah ahbreh/thyehrrah ehl rehstahoorahnteh?

Can we wait for _____
a table?
¿Podemos esperar hasta que se desocupe una mesa?
pohdehmohs ehspehrahr ahstah keh seh dehsohkoopeh oonah mehsah?

Do we have to wait ____
long?
¿Tenemos que esperar mucho?
tehnehmohs keh ehspehrahr moochoh?

Is this seat taken? _____
¿Está ocupada esta silla?
ehstah ohkoopahdah ehstah seelyah?

Could we sit _____
here/there?
¿Podemos sentarnos aquí/allí?
pohdemohs sehntahrnohs ahkee/ahlyee?

Can we sit by the_____
window?
¿Podemos sentarnos junto a la ventana?
pohdehmohs sehntahrnohs hoontoh ah lah behntahnah?

Can we eat outside? ___
¿Podemos comer afuera?
pohdehmohs kohmehr ahfwehrah?

Do you have another ___
chair for us?
¿Podría traernos otra silla?
pohdreeah trahehrnohs ohtrah seelyah?

Do you have a _____
highchair?
¿Podría traernos una silla para niños?
pohdreeah trahehrnohs oonah seelyah pahrah neenyohs?

Is there a socket for ____ this bottle-warmer?	¿Hay un enchufe para este calentador de biberones? *ay oon ehnchoofeh pahrah ehsteh kahlehntahdohr deh beebehrohnehs?*
Could you warm up ____ this bottle/jar for me?	¿Podría calentarme este biberón/este bote? *pohdreeah kahlehntahrmeh ehsteh beebehrohn/ehsteh bohteh?*
Not too hot, please ____	Que no esté muy caliente, por favor *keh noh ehsteh mwee kahlyehnteh pohr fahbohr*
Is there somewhere I ____ can change the baby's nappy?	¿Hay algún lugar para cambiar al bebé? *ay ahlgoon loogahr pahrah kahmbyahr ahl behbeh?*
Where are the toilets? ____	¿Dónde están los servicios? *dohnde ehstahn lohs sehrbeethyohs?*

4.2 Ordering

Waiter! _____	¡Camarero! *kahmahrehroh!*
Madam!/Sir! _____	¡Oiga, (por favor)! *oygah (pohr fahbohr)!*
We'd like something to ___ eat/a drink	Quisiéramos comer/beber algo *keesyehrahmohs kohmehr/behber ahlgoh*
Could I have a quick ____ meal?	¿Podría comer algo rápido? *pohdreeah kohmehr ahlgoh rahpeedoh?*
We don't have much ____ time	Tenemos poco tiempo *tehnehmohs pohkoh tyehmpoh*
We'd like to have a ____ drink first	Antes quisiéramos beber algo *ahntehs keesyehrahmohs behber ahlgoh*
Could we see the _____ menu/wine list, please?	¿Nos podría traer la carta/la carta de vinos? *nohs pohdreeah trahehr lah kahrtah/lah kahrtah deh beenohs?*

Do you have a menu ___ in English?	¿Tienen menú en inglés? *tyehnehn mehnoo ehn eenglehs?*
Do you have a dish ___ of the day?	¿Tienen menú del día/menú turístico? *tyehnehn mehnoo dehl deeah/mehnoo tooreesteekoh?*
We haven't made a ___ choice yet	Todavía no hemos elegido *tohdahbeeah noh ehmohs ehleh<u>h</u>eedoh*
What do you _____ recommend?	¿Qué nos recomienda? *keh nohs rehkohmyehndah?*
What are the _____ specialities of the region/the house?	¿Cuáles son las especialidades de la región/de la casa? *kwahlehs sohn lahs ehspehthyahleedahdehs deh lah reh<u>h</u>yohn/deh lah kahsah?*
I like strawberries/ ___ olives	Me gustan las fresas/las aceitunas *meh goostahn lahs frehsahs/lahs ahtheheetoonahs*
I don't like meat/fish/... _	No me gusta el pescado/la carne/... *noh meh goostah ehl pehskahdoh/lah kahrneh/...*
What's this? _____	¿Qué es esto? *keh ehs ehstoh?*

¿Van a tomar un aperitivo?	Would you like a drink first?
¿Ya han elegido?	Have you decided?
¿Qué van a tomar?	What would you like to eat?
Que aproveche	Enjoy your meal
¿Quiere su bistec rojo, mediano o muy hecho?	Would you like your steak rare, medium or well done?
¿Van a tomar postre/café?	Would you like a dessert/coffee?

Does it have...in it? ____	¿Lleva...? *lyehbah...?*
What does it taste ____ like?	¿A qué sabe? *ah keh sahbeh?*
Is this a hot or a _____ cold dish?	¿Es un plato caliente o frío? *ehs oon plahtoh kahlyehnteh oh freeoh?*
Is this sweet? _____	¿Es un plato dulce? *ehs oon plahtoh doolthe?*
Is this spicy? _____	¿Es un plato picante? *ehs oon plahtoh peekahnteh?*
Do you have anything __ else, please?	¿Tendría otra cosa? *tehndreeah ohtrah kohsah?*
I'm on a salt-free diet __	No puedo comer sal *noh pwehdoh kohmehr sahl*
I can't eat pork _____	No puedo comer carne de cerdo *noh pwehdoh kohmehr kahrneh deh thehrdoh*
– sugar _____	No puedo comer azúcar *noh pwehdo kohmehr ahtookahr*
– fatty foods _____	No puedo comer grasa *noh pwehdoh kohmehr grahsah*
– (hot) spices_____	No puedo comer cosas picantes *noh pwehdoh kohmehr kohsahs peekahntehs*
I'll/we'll have what ____ those people are having	Lo mismo que esos señores, por favor *loh meesmoh keh ehsohs sehnyohrehs pohr fahbohr*
I'd like... _____	Para mí... *pahrah mee...*
We're not having a____ starter	No vamos a comer primer plato *noh bahmohs ah kohmehr preemehr plahtoh*
The child will share ____ what we're having	El niño/la niña comerá de nuestro menú *ehl neenyoh/lah neenyah kohmehrah deh nwehstroh mehnoo*

Could I have some_____ more bread, please?	Más pan, por favor *mahs pahn pohr fahbohr*
– a bottle of water/ _____ wine	Otra botella de agua/de vino, por favor *ohtrah bohtehlyah deh ahgwah/deh beenoh, pohr fahbohr*
– another helping of... __	Otra ración de..., por favor *ohtrah rahthyohn deh..., pohr fahbohr*
– some salt and pepper	¿Podría traerme sal y pimienta? *pohdreeah trahehrmeh sahl ee peemyehntah?*
– a napkin _____	¿Podría traerme una servilleta? *pohdreeah trahehrmeh oonah sehrbeelyehtah?*
– a spoon_____	¿Podría traerme una cuchara? *pohdreeah trahehrmeh oonah koochahrah?*
– an ashtray_____	¿Podría traerme un cenicero? *pohdreeah trahehrmeh oon thehneethehroh?*
– some matches_____	¿Podría traerme unas cerillas? *pohdreeah trahehrmeh oonahs thehreelyahs?*
– some toothpicks _____	¿Podría traerme unos palillos? *pohdreeah trahehrmeh oonohs pahleelyohs?*
– a glass of water_____	¿Podría traerme un vaso de agua? *pohdreeah trahehrmeh oon bahsoh deh ahgwah?*
– a straw (for the child) _	¿Podría traerme una pajita (para el niño/ la niña)? *pohdreeah trahehrmeh oonah pah<u>h</u>eetah (pahrah ehl neenyoh/lah neenyah)?*
Enjoy your meal!_____	¡Que aproveche! *keh ahprohbehcheh!*
You too! _____	Igualmente *eegwahlmehnteh*
Cheers!_____	¡Salud! *sahloodh!*

The next round's _____ on me	La próxima ronda la pago yo
	lah prohxeemah rohndah lah pahgoh yoh
Could we have a _____ doggy bag, please?	¿Podemos llevarnos las sobras?
	pohdehmohs lyehbarnohs lahs sohbrahs?

4.3 The bill

See also 8.2 Settling the bill

How much is _____ this dish?	¿Cuánto vale este plato?
	kwahntoh bahleh ehsteh plahtoh?
Could I have the bill, ___ please?	La cuenta, por favor
	lah kwehntah, pohr fahbohr
All together _____	Todo junto
	tohdoh hoontoh
Everyone pays _____ separately	Cada uno paga lo suyo
	kahdah oonoh pahgah loh sooyoh
Could we have the_____ menu again, please?	¿Podría traernos otra vez la carta?
	pohdreeah trahehrnohs ohtrah behth lah kahrtah?
The...is not on the bill __	Ha olvidado apuntar el/la...
	ah olbeedahdoh ahpoontahr ehl/lah...

4.4 Complaints

It's taking a very _____ long time	Están tardando mucho
	ehstahn tahrdahndoh moochoh
We've been here an ____ hour already	Ya llevamos una hora aquí
	yah lyebahmohs oonah ohrah ahkee
This must be a mistake_	Esto tiene que ser una equivocación
	ehstoh tyehneh keh sehr oonah ehkeebohkahthyohn

This is not what I _____ ordered	Esto no es lo que he pedido *ehstoh noh ehs loh keh eh pehdeedoh*
I ordered... _____	He pedido... *eh pehdeedoh*
There's a dish missing__	Falta un plato *fahltah oon plahtoh*
This is broken/ _____ not clean	Esto está roto/no está limpio *ehstoh ehstah rohtoh/noh ehstah leempyoh*
The food's cold_____	La comida está fría *lah kohmeedah ehstah freeah*
– not fresh _____	La comida no es fresca *lah kohmeedah noh ehs frehskah*
– too salty/sweet/spicy _	La comida está muy salada/dulce/picante *lah kohmeedah ehstah mwee sahlahdah/dooltheh/peekahnteh*
The meat's not done ___	La carne está cruda *lah kahrneh ehstah kroodah*
– overdone _____	La carne está muy hecha *lah kahrneh ehstah mwee ehchah*
– tough_____	La carne está dura *lah kahrneh ehstah doorah*
– off_____	La carne está podrida *lah kahrneh ehstah pohdreedah*
Could I have _____ something else instead of this?	¿Me podría traer otra cosa en lugar de esto? *meh pohdreeah trahehr ohtrah kohsah ehn loogahr deh ehstoh?*
The bill/this amount is__ not right	La cuenta/este precio está mal *lah kwehntah/ehsteh prehthyoh ehstah mahl*
We didn't have this ____	Esto no lo hemos comido/bebido *ehstoh noh loh ehmohs kohmeedoh/behbeedoh*
There's no paper in the _ toilet	No hay papel en el servicio *noh ay pahpehl ehn ehl sehrbeethyoh*
Do you have a _____ complaints book?	¿Tienen libro de quejas? *tyehnen leebroh deh kehhas?*

Will you call the _____ | Haga el favor de llamar al jefe
manager, please? | *ahgah ehl fahbohr deh lyamahr ahl hehfeh*

4.5 Paying a compliment

That was a wonderful __ | Hemos comido muy bien
meal | *ehmohs kohmeedoh mwee byehn*
The food was excellent _ | La comida ha estado exquisita
| *lah kohmeedah ah ehstahdoh ehxkeeseetah*
The...in particular was __ | Sobre todo nos ha gustado el/la...
delicious | *sohbreh tohdoh nohs ah goostahdoh ehl/lah...*

4.6 The menu

aperitivo apéritif	pastelería	postres
aves poultry	pastry	sweets/dessert
azúcar	pescados	primeros platos
sugar	fish	starters
bebidas alcohólicas	platos calientes	raciones
alcoholic beverages	hot dishes	portions
bebidas calientes	platos combinados	servicio incluido
hot beverages	combined dishes	service included
carta de vinos	plato del día	sopas
wine list	dish of the day	soups
cócteles cocktails	platos fríos	tapas
cubierto	cold dishes	tapas
cover charge	platos principales	venado
entremeses variados	main courses	game
hors d'oeuvres	platos típicos	verduras
mariscos seafood	regional specialities	vegetables

4.7 Alphabetical list of drinks and dishes

aceituna
olive

aguacate
avocado

ajo
garlic

albóndigas
meat balls

alcachofa
artichoke

almejas
clams

almendras
almonds

ancas de rana
frog's legs

anchoa/boquerón
anchovy

anguila
eel

anís
aniseed

apio
celery

arenque
herring

arroz
rice

asado
roast, roasted

atún/bonito
tuna

avellana
hazelnut

bacalao
cod

batido de...
milk shake

berenjena
aubergine

biftec
steak

bizcocho (borracho)
sponge cake(with
   sherry or similar)

bocadillo
sandwich

buey/vaca
beef

cabrito
kid

café (solo/con
   leche)
coffee (black/white)

calamares (en su
   tinta)
squid (cooked in their
   ink)

caldo
broth

callos
tripe

cangrejo
crab

caracoles
snails

carne
meat

carpa
carp

castaña
chestnut

cebolla
onion

cerdo
pork

cerezas
cherries

cerveza
beer

chorizo
chorizo (paprika
   flavoured salami
   sausage)

chucrut
sauerkraut

chuleta/costilla
chop

churros
fritters

ciervo
venison

cigalas
Dublin Bay prawns

ciruela
plum

cochinillo asado
roast suckling pig
cocido
boiled
codorniz
quail
col/berza
cabbage
coles de Bruselas
Brussels sprouts
coliflor
cauliflower
coñac
brandy
conejo
rabbit
copa helada/helado
ice cream
cordero
lamb
crema/nata
cream
criadillas/mollejas
sweetbreads
crudo
raw
cuba libre
rum coke
dátil
date
dulce
sweet

emperador
swordfish
en escabeche
pickled
endibia
chicory/endive
ensalada (mixta)
mixed salad
ensaladilla rusa
Russian salad
escalope
escalope
espárragos
asparagus
especies
spices
espinaca
spinach
fideos
noodles
filete
fillet
flan
cream caramel
frambuesa
raspberry
fresa
strawberry
frito
fried
fruta (del tiempo)
seasonal fruit

galleta
biscuit
gambas
prawns
garbanzos
chick peas
gazpacho andaluz
gazpacho (cold
  soup)
granizado de
  limón/café
iced drink
  (lemon/coffee)
grosellas
red/black currants
guisado
stew
guisantes
peas
habas
broad beans
harina
flour
hígado de oca
goose liver
higo
fig
huevos al plato/
  duros/revueltos
fried/hard
  boiled/scrambled
  eggs

jamón de York/serrano
ham (cooked/Parma style)

jerez (seco, dulce)
sherry (dry, sweet)

judías verdes
French beans

jugo/zumo
fruit juice

langosta
lobster

langostino
crayfish

leche
milk

lechuga
lettuce

legumbres
vegetables (legumes)

lengua
tongue

lenguado
sole

lentejas
lentils

licor
liqueur

liebre
hare

limón
lemon

lomo de cerdo
tenderloin of pork

maíz (mazorca)
corn (on the cob)

mantequilla
butter

manzana
apple

mazapán
marzipan

mejillones
mussels

melocotón (en almíbar)
peach (in syrup)

melón
melon

membrillo
quince

merluza
hake

mermelada
jam

mero
sea bass

morcilla
black pudding

mostaza
mustard

muslo de pollo
drumstick

nuez
walnut

ostras
oysters

paella
paella

pan
bread

pastel
cake

patatas fritas
chips/crisps

pato (silvestre)
(wild) duck

pechuga (de pollo)
(chicken) breast

pepino
cucumber

pepinillos
gherkins

pera
pear

perdiz
partridge

perejil
parsley

pescado
fish

picadillo de ternera
minced veal

pierna (de cordero)
leg (of lamb)

pimentón
paprika

pimienta
pepper

pimientos
green/red peppers

piña
pineapple

plancha (a la)
grilled
plátano
banana
plato principal
main course
platos típicos
regional
  specialities
pollo
chicken
puerro
leek
pulpo
octopus
queso
cheese
rábanos
radishes
rabo de buey
oxtail
rape
monkfish
remolacha
beetroot
riñones
kidneys
rodaballo
turbot
romana (a la)
deep fried
vino rosado
rosé wine
salchicha
sausage

salchichón
salami
salmón
salmon
salmón ahumado
smoked salmon
salmonete
red mullet
sandía
water melon
sangría
sangría
sardinas
sardines
setas
mushrooms
solomillo de buey
fillet of beef
sopa
soup
tarta helada
ice cream cake
ternera
veal
tinto
red wine
tocino
bacon
tortilla española
Spanish omelette
  (potato)
tortilla francesa
plain omelette
tortitas
waffles

trucha
trout
trufas
truffles
turrón
nougat
uvas
grapes
verduras
green vegetables
vinagre
vinegar
zanahorias
carrots
zumo de naranja
orange juice

5 On the road

5.1 Asking for directions 63

5.2 Customs 64

5.3 Luggage 66

5.4 Traffic signs 70

5.5 The car 71

   The parts of a car 68

5.6 The petrol station 71

5.7 Breakdown and repairs 72

5.8 The bicycle/moped 75

   The parts of a bicycle 76

5.9 Renting a vehicle 78

5.10 Hitchhiking 79

5.1 Asking for directions

Excuse me, could I ask you something?	Perdone, ¿podría preguntarle algo? *pehrdohneh, pohdreeah prehgoontahrleh ahlgoh?*
I've lost my way	Me he perdido *meh eh pehrdeedoh*
Is there a(n)... around here?	¿Sabe dónde hay un(a)...por aquí? *sahbeh dohndeh ay oon(ah)...pohr ahkee?*
Is this the way to...?	¿Se va por aquí a...? *seh bah pohr ahkee ah...?*
Could you tell me how to get to the... (name of place) by car/on foot?	¿Podría decirme cómo llegar a... (en coche/a pie)? *pohdreeah dehtheermeh kohmoh lyehgahr ah... (ehn kohcheh/ah pyeh)?*
What's the quickest way to...?	¿Cómo hago para llegar lo antes posible a...? *kohmoh ahgoh pahrah lyehgahr loh ahntehs pohseebleh ah...?*
How many kilometres is it to...?	¿Cuántos kilómetros faltan para llegar a...? *kwahntohs keelohmehtrohs fahltahn pahrah lyehgahr ah...?*
Could you point it out on the map?	¿Podría señalarlo en el mapa? *pohdreeah sehnyahlahrloh ehn ehl mahpah?*

No sé; no soy de aquí	I don't know, I don't know my way around here
Por aquí no es	You're going the wrong way
Tiene que volver a...	You have to go back to...
Allí los carteles le indicarán	From there on just follow the signs
Vuelva a preguntar allí	When you get there, ask again

todo recto	la calle	el viaducto
straight ahead	the street	the fly-over
a la izquierda	el semáforo	el puente
left	the traffic light	the bridge
a la derecha	el túnel	el paso a nivel/las
right	the tunnel	barreras
doblar	el stop	the level crossing/the
turn	the `give way' sign	boom gates
seguir	el edificio	el cartel en dirección
follow	the building	de...
cruzar	en la esquina	the sign pointing to...
cross	at the corner	la flecha
el cruce	el río	the arrow
the intersection	the river	

5.2 Customs

● **Border documents:** along with your passport you must carry your original valid full driving licence (together with paper counterpart if photocard licence), vehicle registration document and motor insurance certificate. Contact your motor insurer for advice at least a month before taking your vehicle overseas to ensure that you are covered. There is no restriction, either by quantity or value, on goods purchased by travellers from another EU country provided they are for their own personal use. Guidelines have been published. As these are subject to change you are advised to contact your travel agent, customs or the Embassy for further details before travelling.

My children are entered on this passport	Mis hijos están apuntados en este pasaporte
	mees eehohs ehstahn ahpoontahdohs ehn ehsteh pahsahpohrteh
I'm travelling through___	Estoy de paso
	ehstoy deh pahsoh

Su pasaporte, por favor	Your passport, please
La tarjeta verde, por favor	Your green card, please
El permiso de circulación/la carta gris, por favor	Your vehicle documents, please
¿Adónde va?	Where are you heading?
¿Cuánto tiempo piensa quedarse?	How long are you planning to stay?
¿Tiene algo que declarar?	Do you have anything to declare?
¿Puede abrir esto?	Open this, please

I'm going on holiday to... — Voy de vacaciones a...
boy deh bahkahthyohnehs ah...

I'm on a business trip — He venido en viaje de negocios
eh behneedoh ehn byah<u>h</u>heh deh nehgohthyohs

I don't know how long I'll be staying yet — Todavía no sé cuánto tiempo me quedaré
tohdahbeeah noh seh kwahntoh tyehmpoh meh kehdahreh

I'll be staying here for a weekend — Pienso quedarme un fin de semana
pyehnsoh kehdahrmeh oon feen deh sehmahnah

– for a few days — Pienso quedarme unos días
pyehnsoh kehdahrmeh oonohs deeahs

– for a week — Pienso quedarme una semana
pyehnsoh kehdahrmeh oonah sehmahnah

– for two weeks — Pienso quedarme dos semanas
pyehnsoh kehdahrmeh dohs sehmahnahs

I've got nothing to declare — No tengo nada que declarar
noh tehngoh nahdah keh dehklahrahr

I've got...with me — Traigo...
trahygoh...

– ...cartons of _____ cigarettes	Traigo...cartones de cigarrillos *trahygoh...kahrtohnehs deh theegahrreelyohs*
– ...bottles of... _____	Traigo...botellas de... *trahygoh...bohtehlyahs deh...*
– some souvenirs _____	Traigo algunos recuerdos de viaje *trahygoh ahlgoonohs rehkwehrdohs de byahhheh*
These are personal _____ effects	Estos son artículos personales *ehstohs sohn ahrteekoolohs pehrsohnahlehs*
These are not new _____	Estas cosas no son nuevas *ehstahs kohsahs noh sohn nwehbahs*
Here's the receipt _____	Aquí está el recibo *ahkee ehstah ehl rehtheeboh*
This is for private use __	Esto es para uso personal *ehstoh ehs pahrah oosoh pehrsohnahl*
How much import duty _ do I have to pay?	¿Cuánto tengo que pagar por derechos de aduana? *kwahntoh tehngoh keh pahgahr pohr dehrehchohs deh ahdwahnah?*
Can I go now? _____	¿Puedo seguir? *pwehdoh sehgheer?*

5.3 Luggage

Porter! _____	¡Mozo! *mohthoh!*
Could you take this _____ luggage to...?	¿Podría llevar este equipaje a...? *pohdreeah lyehbahr ehsteh ehkeepahhheh ah...?*
How much do I _____ owe you?	¿Cuánto le debo? *kwahntoh leh dehboh?*

Where can I find a _____ luggage trolley?
¿Dónde hay carritos para el equipaje?
dohndeh ay kahrreetohs pahrah ehl ehkeepah<u>h</u>eh?

Could you store this ___ luggage for me?
¿Podría dejar este equipaje en la consigna?
pohdreeah deh<u>h</u>ar ehsteh ehkeepah<u>h</u>eh ehn lah kohnseegnah?

Where are the luggage _ lockers?
¿Dónde está la consigna automática?
dohndeh ehstah lah kohnseegnah ahootohmahteekah?

I can't get the locker ___ open
No logro abrir la puerta de la consigna
noh lohgroh ahbreer lah pwehrtah deh lah kohnseegnah

How much is it _____ per item per day?
¿Cuánto sale por bulto y por día?
kwahntoh sahleh pohr booltoh ee pohr deeah?

This is not my bag/ _____ suitcase
Este/ésta no es mi bolso/mi maleta
ehsteh/ehstah noh ehs mee bohlsoh/mee mahlehtah

There's one item/bag/ __ suitcase missing still
Todavía falta un bulto/un bolso/una maleta
tohdahbeeah fahltah oon booltoh/oon bohlsoh/oonah mahlehtah

My suitcase is_____ damaged
Me han dañado la maleta
meh ahn dahnyahdoh lah mahlehtah

The parts of a car

battery	la batería	*lah bahtehreeah*
rear light	el faropiloto	*ehl fahroh peelohtoh*
rear-view mirror	el retrovisor	*ehl rehtrohbeesohr*
reversing light	la luz de marcha atrás	*lah looth deh mahrchah ahtrahs*
aerial	la antena	*lah ahntehnah*
car radio	la autorradio	*lah ahootohrrahdyoh*
petrol tank	el depósito de gasolina	*ehl dehpohseetoh deh gahsohleenah*
inside mirror	el espejo interior	*ehl ehspehhoh eentehreeohr*
sparking plugs	las bujías	*lahs booheeahs*
fuel filter/pump	el separador de gasolina	*ehl sehpahrahdohr deh gahsohleenah*
wing mirror	el espejo exterior	*ehl ehspehoh ehxtehryohr*
bumper	el parachoques	*ehl pahrahchohkehs*
carburettor	el carburador	*ehl kahrboorahdohr*
crankcase	el cárter	*ehl kahrtehr*
cylinder	el cilindro	*ehl theeleendroh*
ignition	los contactos del ruptor	*lohs kohntahktohs dehl rooptohr*
warning light	la luz piloto	*lah looth peelohtoh*
dynamo	la dinamo	*lah deenahmoh*
accelerator	el pedal del acelerador	*ehl pehdahl dehl ahthehlehrahdohr*
handbrake	el freno de mano	*ehl frehnoh deh mahnoh*
valve	la válvula	*lah bahlboolah*
silencer	el silenciador	*ehl seelehnthyahdohr*
boot	el maletero	*ehl mahlehtehroh*
headlight	el faro	*ehl fahroh*
crank shaft	el cigueñal	*ehl theegwehnyahl*
air filter	el filtro de aire	*ehl feeltroh deh ayreh*
fog lamp	la luz antiniebla trasera	*llah looth ahnteenyehblah trahsehrah*
engine block	el bloque motor	*ehl blohkeh mohtohr*

camshaft	el árbol de levas	ehl ahrbohl deh lehbahs
oil filter/pump	el filtro de aceitela	ehl feeltroh deh ahtheheeteh
dipstick	la varilla indicadora de nivel de aceite	lah bahreelyah eendeekahdohrah deh neebehl deh ahtheyteh
pedal	el pedal	ehl pehdahl
door	la portezuela	lah pohrtehthwehlah
radiator	el radiador	ehl rahdyahdohr
brake disc	el disco del freno	ehl deeskoh dehl frehnoh
spare wheel	la rueda de reserva	lah rwehdah deh rehsehrbah
indicator	el intermitente	ehl eentehrmeetehnteh
steering wheel	el volante	ehl bohlahnteh
windscreen wiper	el limpiaparabrisas	ehl leempyahpahrahbreesahs
shock absorbers	los amortiguadores	lohs ahmohrteegwahdohrehs
sunroof	el techo corredizo	ehl tehchoh kohrrehdeethoh
spoiler	el spoiler	ehl spoheelehr
starter motor	el motor de arranque	ehl mohtohr deh ahrrahnkeh
steering column	el cárter de la dirección	ehl kahrtehr deh lah deerehkthyohn
exhaust pipe	el tubo de escape	ehl tooboh deh ehskahpeh
seat belt	el cinturón de seguridad	ehl theentoorohn deh sehgooreedahdh
fan	el ventilador	ehl behnteelahdohr
distributor cables	los cables del distribuidor	lohs kahblehs dehl deestreebweedohr
gear lever	la palanca de cambios	lah pahlahnkah deh kahmbyohs
windscreen	el parabrisas	ehl pahrahbreesahs
water pump	la bomba de agua	lah bohmbah deh ahgwah
wheel	la rueda	lah rwehdah
hubcap	el tapacubos	ehl tahpahkoobohs
piston	el émbolo	ehl ehmbohloh

5.4 Traffic signs

a la derecha	ceda el paso	obras
right	give way	roadworks ahead
a la izquierda	cerrado	paso a nivel
left	closed	(sin barreras)
abierto	cruce peligroso	level crossing
open	dangerous crossing	(no gates)
altura máxima	curvas en ... km	paso de ganado
maximum height	bends for...km	cattle crossing
arcenes sin afirmar	despacio	peaje
soft verges	drive slowly	toll
¡atención, peligro!	desprendimientos	peatones
danger	loose rocks	pedestrian crossing
autopista de peaje	desvío	precaución
toll road	diversion	caution
autovía	dirección prohibida	prohibido aparcar
motorway	no entry	no parking
bajada peligrosa	dirección única	prohibido adelantar
steep hill	one-way traffic	no overtaking
calzada resbaladiza	encender las luces	puesto de socorro
slippery road	switch on lights	first aid
cambio de sentido	espere	salida
change of direction	wait	exit
cañada	estacionamiento	salida de camiones
animals crossing	reglamentado	factory/works exit
carretera comarcal	limited parking zone	substancias
secondary road	excepto...	peligrosas
carretera cortada	except for...	dangerous
road closed	fin de...	substances
carretera en mal	end of...	travesía peligrosa
estado	hielo	dangerous crossing
irregular road surface	ice on road	zona peatonal
carretera nacional	niebla	pedestrian zone
main road	beware fog	

5.5 The car

● **The motorways** in Spain have been very well updated and expanded. Tolls, however, can be expensive.

Particular traffic regulations:
– maximum speed for cars: 120km/h on toll roads, 110km/h on other motorways, 90km/h outside built-up areas, 50km/h in built-up areas
– give way: all traffic from the right has the right of way, except for major roads and thoroughfares.

It is compulsory to carry a spare set of bulbs and a warning triangle. Drivers and/or passengers must wear a reflective jacket when exiting a car which has broken down on a motorway or main or busy road.

5.6 The petrol station

● **Petrol is easily available** but rather expensive in Spain.

How many kilometres __ to the next petrol station, please?	¿Cuántos kilómetros faltan para la próxima gasolinera? *kwahntohs keelohmehtrohs fahltahn pahrah lah prohxeemah gahsohleenehrah?*
I would like...litres of..., _ please	Póngame...litros de..., por favor *pohngahmeh...leetrohs deh..., pohr fahbohr*
– super _____	Póngame...litros de gasolina súper *pohngahmeh...leetrohs de gahsohleenah soopehr*
– leaded _____	Póngame...litros de gasolina normal *pohngahmeh...leetrohs deh gahsohleenah nohrmahl*
– unleaded_____	Póngame...litros de gasolina sin plomo *pohngahmeh...leetrohs deh gahsohleenah seen plohmoh*

– diesel_____	Póngame...litros de gasóleo
	pohngahmeh...leetrohs deh gahsohlehoh
I would like...euros' ____ worth of petrol, please	Póngame gasolina por...euros
	pohngahmeh gahsohleenah pohr...euros
Fill her up, please_____	Lléneme el depósito, por favor
	lyehnehmeh ehl dehpohseetoh, pohr fahvohr
Could you check...?____	¿Podría controlar...?
	pohdreeah kohntrohlahr?
– the oil level_____	¿Podría controlar el nivel del aceite?
	pohdreeah kohntrohlahr ehl neebehl dehl ahtheheeteh?
– the tyre pressure_____	¿Podría controlar la presión de los neumáticos?
	pohdreeah kohntrohlahr lah prehsyohn deh lohs nehoomahteekohs?
Could you change the__ oil, please?	¿Podría cambiar el aceite?
	pohdreeah kahmbyahr ehl atheheeteh?
Could you clean the ___ windows/the windscreen, please?	¿Podría limpiar los cristales/el parabrisas?
	pohdreeah leempyahr lohs kreestahlehs/ehl pahrahbreesahs?
Could you give the car _ a wash, please?	¿Podría lavar el coche?
	pohdreeah lahbahr ehl kohcheh?

5.7 Breakdown and repairs

I'm having car trouble. _ Could you give me a hand?	Tengo una avería. ¿Podría ayudarme?
	tehngoh oonah ahbehreeah. pohdreeah ahyoodahrmeh?
I've run out of petrol ___	Me he quedado sin gasolina
	meh eh kehdahdoh seen gahsohleenah

I've locked the keys in the car
Me he dejado las llaves en el coche
meh eh de<u>h</u>hahdoh lahs lyabehs ehn ehl kohcheh

The car/motorbike/ moped won't start
El coche/la moto/el ciclomotor no arranca
ehl kohcheh/lah mohtoh/ehl theeklohmohtohr noh ahrrahnkah

Could you contact the recovery service for me, please?
¿Podría avisar al auxilio en carretera?
pohdreeah ahbeesar ahl ahooxeelyoh ehn kahrrehtehrah?

Could you call a garage for me, please?
¿Podría llamar por teléfono a un taller mecánico?
pohdreeah lyahmahr pohr tehlehfohnoh ah oon tahlyehr mehkahneekoh?

Could you give me a lift to...?
¿Me podría llevar a...?
meh pohdreeah lyehbahr ah...?

– a garage/into town?
¿Me podría llevar a un taller mecánico/a la ciudad?
meh pohdreeah lyehbahr ah oon tahlyehr mehkahneekoh/ah lah thyoodahdh?

– a phone booth?
¿Me podría llevar a una cabina de teléfonos?
meh pohdreeah lyehbahr ah oonah kahbeenah deh tehlehfohnohs?

– an emergency phone?
¿Me podría llevar a un teléfono de emergencia?
meh pohdreeah lyehbahr ah oon tehlehfohnoh deh ehmehr<u>h</u>ehnthyah?

Can we take my bicycle/moped?
¿Podríamos llevar la bicicleta/el ciclomotor?
pohdreeahmohs lyehbahr lah beetheeklehtah/ehl theeklohmohtohr?

Could you tow me to a garage?
¿Podría remolcarme hasta un taller mecánico?
pohdreeah rehmohlkahrmeh ahstah oon tahlyehr mehkahneekoh?

73

There's probably _____ something wrong with...(See 5.8).	Me parece que está fallando el/la... *meh pahrehtheh keh ehstah fahlyahndoh ehl/lah...*
Can you fix it? _____	¿Podría arreglarlo? *pohdreeah ahrrehglahrloh?*
Could you fix my tyre? _	¿Podría arreglar el neumático? *pohdreeah ahrrehglahr ehl nehoomahteekoh?*
Could you change this _ wheel?	¿Podría cambiar esta rueda? *pohdreeah kahmbyahr ehstah rwehdah?*
Can you fix it so it'll____ get me to...?	¿Podría arreglarlo de tal manera que pueda seguir hasta...? *pohdreeah ahrrehglahrloh deh tahl mahnehrah keh pwehdah sehgheer ahstah...?*
Which garage can _____ help me?	¿En qué taller me podrán ayudar entonces? *ehn keh tahlyehr meh pohdrahn ahyoodahr ehntohnthehs?*
When will my _____ car/bicycle be ready?	¿Para cuándo estará mi coche/bicicleta? *pahrah kwahndoh ehstahrah mee kohcheh/beetheeklehtah?*
Can I wait for it here? _	¿Puedo esperar aquí? *pwehdoh ehspehrahr ahkee?*
How much will it cost? _	¿Por cuánto me va a salir? *pohr kwahntoh meh bah ah sahleer?*
Could you itemise _____ the bill?	¿Podría especificar la cuenta? *pohdreeah ehspehtheefeekahr lah kwehntah?*
Can I have a receipt ___ for the insurance?	¿Me podría dar un recibo para el seguro? *meh pohdreeah dahr oon rehtheeboh pahrah ehl sehgooroh?*

5.8 The bicycle/moped

● **Cycle paths** are rare in Spain. Not much consideration for bikes should be expected on the roads. The maximum speed for mopeds is 40km/h both inside and outside town centres. A helmet is compulsory.

No tengo piezas de recambio para su coche/su bicicleta	I don't have parts for your car/bicycle
Las piezas de recambio me las tienen que traer de otro sitio	I have to get the parts from somewhere else
Las piezas de recambio tengo que encargarlas	I have to order the parts
Eso llevará medio día	That'll take half a day
Eso llevará un día	That'll take a day
Eso llevará unos días	That'll take a few days
Eso llevará una semana	That'll take a week
Su coche ha quedado totalmente destruido	Your car is a write-off
Ya no se puede hacer nada para arreglarlo	It can't be repaired.
El coche/la moto/el ciclomotor/la bicicleta estará para las...	The car/motor bike/moped/bicycle will be ready at... o'clock.

The parts of a bicycle

rear lamp	el piloto	*ehl peelohtoh*
rear wheel	la rueda trasera	*lah rwehdah trahsehrah*
(luggage) carrier	el portaequipajes	*ehl pohrtahehkeepahhehs*
bicycle fork	la cabeza	*lah kahbehthah*
bell	el timbre	*ehl teembreh*
inner tube	la cámara	*lah kahmahrah*
tyre	el neumático/la cubierta	*ehl nehoomahteekoh/lah koobyehrtah*
crank	la biela	*lah byehlah*
gear change	el cambio de velocidades	*ehl kahmbyoh deh behlotheedahdehs*
wire	el hilo	*ehl eeloh*
dynamo	la dinamo	*lah deenahmoh*
bicycle trailer	el remolque de bicicleta	*ehl rehmohlkeh deh beetheeklehtah*
frame	el cuadro	*ehl kwahdroh*
dress guard	el guardafaldas	*ehl gwardahfahldahs*
chain	la cadena de rodillos	*lah kahdehnah deh rohdeelyohs*
chain guard	el cubrecadena/el cárter	*ehl koobrehkahdehnah/ehl kahrtehr*
chain lock	la cadena antirrobo	*lah kahdehnah ahnteerrohboh*
milometer	el contador kilométrico	*ehl kohntahdohr keelohmehtreekoh*
child's seat	el sillín para niños	*ehl seelyeen pahrah neenyohs*
headlamp	el faro	*ehl fahroh*
bulb	la bombilla	*lah bohmbeelyah*
pedal	el pedal	*ehl pehdahl*
pump	la bombilla	*lah bohmbeelyah*
reflector	el cristal reflectante	*ehl kreestahl rehflehktahnteh*

brake pad	la zapatilla del freno	*lah thahpahteelyah dehl frehnoh*
brake cable	el cable del freno	*ehl kahbleh dehl frehnoh*
ring lock	la cerradura	*lah thehrrahdoorah*
carrier straps	las bandas elásticas	*lahs bahndahs ehlahsteekahs*
spoke	el radio/el rayo	*ehl rahdyoh/ehl rayoh*
mudguard	el guardabarros	*ehl gwahrdahbahrrohs*
handlebar	el manillar	*ehl mahneelyahr*
chain wheel	el piñón	*ehl peenyohn*
toe clip	el calapiés	*ehl kahlahpyehs*
crank axle	el eje del cigueñal	*ehl ehheh dehl theegwehnyal*
drum brake	el freno de tambor	*ehl frehnoh deh tahmbohr*
tube	la llanta	*lah lyahntah*
valve	la válvula	*lah bahlboolah*
valve tube	el tubo de la válvula	*ehl tooboh deh lah bahlboolah*
gear cable	el cable de velocidades	*ehl kahbleh deh behlohtheedahdehs*
fork	la horquilla	*lah ohrkeelyah*
front wheel	la rueda delantera	*lah rwehdah dehlahntehrah*
seat	el sillín	*el seelyeen*

5.9 Renting a vehicle

I'd like to rent a... _____	Quisiera alquilar un...
	keesyehrah ahlkeelahr oon...
Do I need a (special) ___ licence for that?	¿Hace falta un permiso de conducir (especial)?
	ahtheh fahltah oon pehrmeesoh deh kohndootheer (ehspehthyahl)?
I'd like to rent the...for...	Quisiera alquilar el/la...por...
	keesyehrah ahlkeelahr ehl/lah...pohr...
– one day _____	Quisiera alquilar el/la...por un día
	keesyehrah ahlkeelahr ehl/lah...pohr oon deeah
– two days _____	Quisiera alquilar el/la...por dos días
	keesyehrah ahlkeelahr ehl/lah...pohr dohs deeahs
How much is that per ___ day/week?	¿Cuánto sale por día/semana?
	kwahntoh sahleh pohr deeah/pohr sehmahnah?
How much is the _____ deposit?	¿Cuánto es la fianza?
	kwahntoh ehs lah fyahnthah?
Could I have a receipt___ for the deposit?	¿Me podría dar un recibo por el pago de la fianza?
	meh pohdreeah dahr oon rehtheeboh pohr ehl pahgoh deh lah fyahnthah?
How much is the _____ surcharge per kilometre?	¿Cuánto hay que pagar extra por kilómetro?
	kwahntoh ay keh pahgahr ehxtrah pohr keelohmehtroh?
Does that include_____ petrol?	¿Está incluida la gasolina?
	ehstah eenklooeedah lah gahsohleenah?
Does that include_____ insurance?	¿Está incluido el seguro?
	ehstah eenklooeedoh ehl sehgooroh?

What time can I pick the...up tomorrow?	¿A qué hora puedo pasar mañana a buscar el/la...?
	ah keh ohrah pwehdoh pahsahr mahnyahnah ah booskahr ehl/lah...?
When does the...have to be back?	¿A qué hora tengo que devolver el/la...?
	ah keh ohrah tehngoh keh dehbohlbehr ehl/lah...?
Where's the petrol tank?	¿Dónde está el depósito de gasolina?
	dohndeh ehstah ehl dehpohseetoh deh gahsohleenah?
What sort of fuel does it take?	¿Qué tipo de combustible hay que echarle?
	keh teepoh deh kohmboosteebleh ay keh ehchahrleh?

5.10 Hitchhiking

Where are you heading?	¿Adónde va?
	ahdohndeh bah?
Can I come along?	¿Me podría llevar?
	meh pohdreeah lyehbahr?
Can my boyfriend/ girlfriend come too?	¿Podría llevar también a mi amigo/amiga?
	pohdreeah lyehbahr tahmbyehn ah mee ahmeegoh/ahmeegah?
I'm trying to get to...	Voy a...
	boy ah...
Is that on the way to...?	¿Eso está camino de...?
	ehsoh ehstah kahmeenoh deh...?
Could you drop me off...?	¿Me podría dejar...?
	meh pohdreeah dehhahr...?
– here?	¿Me podría dejar aquí mismo?
	meh pohdreeah dehhahr ahkee meesmoh?

– at the...exit? _____   ¿Me podría dejar en la salida de...?
meh pohdreeah dehhahr ehn lah sahleedah deh...?

– in the centre? _____   ¿Me podría dejar en el centro?
meh pohdreeah dehhahr ehn ehl thehntroh?

– at the next _____   ¿Me podría dejar en la próxima rotonda?
roundabout?   *meh pohdreeah dehhahr ehn lah prohxeemah rohtohndah?*

Could you stop here, ___   ¿Podría pararse aquí?
please?   *pohdreeah pahrahrseh ahkee?*

I'd like to get out here __   Quisiera bajarme aquí
keesyehrah bahhahrmeh ahkee

Thanks for the lift _____   Gracias por llevarme
grahthyahs pohr lyehbahrmeh

6

Public transport

6.1 In general 82

6.2 Questions to passengers 84

6.3 Tickets 85

6.4 Information 87

6.5 Aeroplanes 89

6.6 Trains 89

6.7 Taxis 90

6.1 In general

● **The rail network** has been substantially overhauled and expanded and there is now a good, fast service available with the Talgo and Ave in the south. These trains require payment of a supplement and it is advisable to reserve seats in advance, at the station or at travel agencies. Tickets for buses and the metro can be bought at an *estanco*, as well as metro stations.

Announcements

El tren [de las 10.40] con destino a..., ..., saldrá con (unos)...minutos de retraso	The [10.40] train to...has been delayed by 15 minutes
Por la vía 5 entrará el tren [de las 10.40] con destino a.../procedente de...	The train now arriving at platform 5 is the [10.40] train to .../from...
En la vía 5 está por partir el tren [de las 10.40]...	The [10.40] train to...is about to leave from platform 5
Su atención, por favor Manténganse lejos de la vía; un tren Intercity pasará por la plataforma...	Attention please! Keep your distance from the rail track, an intercity train will pass on platform...
Nos estamos aproximando a la estación de...	We're now approaching...

Where does this train go to?	¿Adónde va este tren?	
	ahdohndeh bah ehsteh trehn?	
Does this boat go to...?	¿Este barco va a...?	
	ehsteh bahrkoh bah ah...?	
Can I take this bus to...?	¿Puedo coger este autobús para ir a...?	
	pwehdoh kohhehr ehsteh ahootohboos pahrah eer ah...?	

Does this train stop at...?	¿Este tren para en...?
	ehsteh trehn pahrah ehn...?
Is this seat taken/free/reserved?	¿Está ocupado/libre/reservado este asiento?
	ehstah ohkoopahdoh/leebreh/ rehsehrbahdoh ehsteh ahsyehntoh?
I've booked...	He reservado...
	eh rehsehrbahdoh...
Could you tell me where I have to get off for... ?	¿Me podría decir dónde me tengo que bajar para ir a...?
	meh pohdreeah dehtheer dohndeh meh tehngoh keh bahhar pahrah eer ah...?
Could you let me know when we get to...?	¿Me podría avisar cuando lleguemos a...?
	meh pohdreeah ahbeesahr kwahndoh lyehghehmohs ah...?
Could you stop at the next stop, please?	La próxima parada, por favor
	lah prohxeemah pahrahdah pohr fahbohr
Where are we now?	¿Dónde estamos?
	dohndeh ehstahmohs?
Do I have to get off here?	¿Tengo que bajarme aquí?
	tehngoh keh bahhahrmeh ahkee?
Have we already passed...?	¿Ya hemos pasado...?
	yah ehmohs pahsahdoh...?
How long have I been asleep?	¿Cuánto tiempo he dormido?
	kwahntoh tyehmpoh eh dohrmeedoh?
How long does... stop here?	¿Cuánto tiempo se queda aquí...?
	kwahntoh tyehmpoh seh kehdah ahkee?
Can I come back on the same ticket?	¿Este billete me sirve para volver?
	ehsteh beelyehteh meh seerbeh pahrah bohlbehr?
Can I change on this ticket?	¿Se puede hacer trasbordo con este billete?
	seh pwehdeh ahthehr trahsbohrdoh kohn ehsteh beelyehteh?
How long is this ticket valid for?	¿Hasta cuándo es válido este billete?
	ahstah kwahndoh ehs bahleedoh ehsteh beelyehteh

How much is the _____ supplement for the Talgo/Ave (high speed train)?	¿Cuánto vale el suplemento para el Talgo/el Ave? _kwahntoh bahleh ehl sooplehmehntoh pahrah ehl tahlgoh/ehl ahbeh?_

6.2 Questions to passengers

Ticket types

¿Primera o segunda clase?	First or second class?
¿Billete de ida o de ida y vuelta?	Single or return?
¿Fumadores o no fumadores?	Smoking or non-smoking?
¿Ventanilla o pasillo?	Window or aisle?
¿Adelante o atrás?	Front or back?
¿Asiento o litera?	Seat or couchette?
¿Arriba, en el medio o abajo?	Top, middle or bottom?
¿Clase turista o preferente?	Tourist class or business class?
¿Camarote o butaca?	Cabin or seat?
¿Individual o doble?	Single or double?
¿Cuántas personas viajan?	How many are travelling?

Destination

¿Adónde quiere ir?	Where are you travelling?
¿Qué día sale?	When are you leaving?
Su...sale a las...	Your...leaves at...
Tiene que hacer trasbordo	You have to change trains
Tiene que bajarse en...	You have to get off at...
Tiene que pasar por...	You have to travel via...
El viaje de ida es el día...	The outward journey is on...
El viaje de vuelta es el día...	The return journey is on...
Tiene que embarcar a las...a más tardar	You have to be on board by...

Inside the vehicle

Billetes, por favor	Your ticket, please
Su reserva, por favor	Your reservation, please
Su pasaporte, por favor	Your passport, please
Se ha equivocado de asiento	You're in the wrong seat
Se ha equivocado de...	You're on/in the wrong...
Este asiento está reservado	This seat is reserved
Tiene que pagar un suplemento	You'll have to pay a supplement
El...tiene un retraso de...minutos	The...has been delayed by...minutes

6.3 Tickets

Where can I...?	¿Dónde...?
	dohndeh...?
– buy a ticket?	¿Dónde se compran los billetes?
	dohndeh seh kohmprahn lohs beelyehtehs?
– make a reservation?	¿Dónde se hacen las reservas?
	dohndeh seh ahtehn lahs rehsehrbahs?
– book a flight?	¿Dónde puedo hacer una reserva para un vuelo?
	dohndeh pwehdoh ahtehr oonah rehsehrbah pahrah oon bwehloh?
Could I have a...to..., please?	Quiero un/una...a...
	kyehroh oon/oonah...ah...
– a single	Quiero un billete de ida a...
	kyehroh oon beelyehteh deh eedah ah...
– a return	Quiero un billete de ida y vuelta a...
	kyehroh oon beelyehteh deh eedah ee bwehltah ah...

first class _____	en primera clase
	ehn preemehrah klahseh
second class _____	en segunda clase
	ehn sehgoondah klahseh
tourist class _____	en clase turista
	ehn klahseh tooreestah
business class _____	en clase preferente
	ehn klahseh prehfehrehnteh
I'd like to book a _____ seat/couchette/cabin	Quisiera reservar un asiento/una litera/un camarote
	keesyehrah rehsehrbahr oon ahsyehntoh/oonah leetehrah/oon kahmahrohteh
I'd like to book a berth _ in the sleeping car	Quisiera reservar una plaza en un coche cama
	keesyehrah rehsehrbahr oonah plahthah ehn oon kohcheh kahmah
top/middle/bottom _____	arriba/en el medio/abajo
	ahrreebah/ehn ehl mehdyoh/ahbahhoh
smoking/no smoking ___	fumadores/no fumadores
	foomahdohrehs/noh foomahdohrehs
by the window _____	ventanilla
	behntahneelyah
single/double _____	individual/doble
	eendeebeedwahl/dohbleh
at the front/back _____	adelante/atrás
	ahdehlahnteh/ahtrahs
There are...of us _____	Somos...personas
	sohmohs...pehrsohnahs
a car _____	un coche
	oon kohcheh
a caravan _____	una caravana
	oonah kahrahbahnah
...bicycles _____	...bicicletas
	...beetheeklehtahs
Do you also have...? ___	¿Tienen...?
	tyehnehn...?

– season tickets? _____	¿Tienen billetes para varios viajes?	
	tyehnen beelyehtehs pahrah bahryohs byahhehs?	
– weekly tickets? _____	¿Tienen abonos semanales?	
	tyehnehn ahbohnohs sehmahnahlehs?	
– monthly season _____ tickets?	¿Tienen abonos mensuales?	
	tyehnehn ahbohnohs mehnswahlehs?	

6.4 Information

Where's-? _____	¿Dónde hay...?
	dohndeh ay...?
Where's the information desk?	¿Dónde está la oficina de información?
	dohndeh ehstah lah ohfeetheenah deh eenfohrmahthyohn?
Where can I find a _____ timetable?	¿Dónde hay un horario?
	dohndeh ay oon ohrahryoh?
Where's the...desk? _____	¿Dónde está el mostrador de...?
	dohndeh ehstah ehl mohstrahdohr deh...?
Do you have a city map with the bus/the underground routes on it?	¿Tendría un plano de la ciudad con la red de autobuses/metro?
	tehndreeah oon plahnoh deh lah thyoodahdh kohn lah rehth deh ahootohboosehs/mehtroh?
Do you have a _____ timetable?	¿Tendría un horario?
	tehndreeah oon ohrahryoh?
I'd like to confirm/ _____ cancel/change my booking for/trip to...	Quisiera confirmar/cancelar/cambiar mi reserva/mi viaje a...
	keesyehrah kohnfeermahr/kahnthehlahr/kahmbyahr mee rehsehrbah/mee byahheh ah...
Will I get my money _____ back?	¿Me devuelven el dinero?
	meh dehbwehlbehn ehl deenehroh?

I want to go to... _____ How do I get there? (What's the quickest way there?)	Tengo que ir a...¿Cómo hago para llegar (lo más rápido posible)? *tehngoh keh eer ah...kohmoh ahgoh pahrah lyehgahr(loh mahs rahpeedoh pohseebleh)?*
How much is a _____ single/return to...?	¿Cuánto vale un billete de ida/de ida y vuelta a...? *kwahntoh bahleh oon beelyehteh deh eedah ee bwehltah ah...?*
Do I have to pay a _____ supplement?	¿Tengo que pagar algún suplemento? *tehngoh keh pahgahr ahlgoon sooplehmehntoh?*
Can I interrupt my _____ journey with this ticket?	¿Con este billete puedo hacer una parada intermedia? *kohn ehsteh beelyehteh pwehdoh ahthehr oonah pahrahdah eentehrmehdyah?*
How much luggage _____ am I allowed?	¿Cuánto equipaje puedo llevar? *kwahntoh ehkeepahheh pwehdoh lyebahr?*
Can I send my luggage_ in advance?	¿Puedo enviar mi equipaje por anticipado? *pwehdoh ehnbeeahr mee ehkeepahheh pohr ahnteetheepahdoh?*
Does this...travel direct?	¿Este...va directo? *ehsteh...bah deerehktoh?*
Do I have to change? __ Where?	¿Tengo que hacer trasbordo? ¿Dónde? *tehngoh keh ahthehr trahsbohrdoh? dohndeh?*
Will there be any _____ stopovers?	¿Habrá escalas? *ahbrah ehskahlahs?*
Does the boat call in at_ any ports on the way?	¿El barco hace alguna escala? *ehl bahrkoh ahtheh ahlgoonah ehskahlah?*
Does the train/ _____ bus stop at...?	¿Este tren/este autobús para en...? *ehsteh trehn/ehsteh ahootohboos pahrah ehn...?*
Where should I get off?_	¿Dónde me tengo que bajar? *dohndeh meh tehngoh keh bahhahr?*

Is there a connection___ to...?	¿Hay enlace para...? *ay ehnlahtheh pahrah...?*
How long do I have to__ wait?	¿Cuánto tengo que esperar? *kwahntoh tehngoh keh ehspehrahr?*
When does...leave? ____	¿Cuándo sale...? *kwahndoh sahleh...?*
What time does the ____ first/next/last...leave?	¿A qué hora sale el primer/próximo/último...? *ah keh ohrah sahleh ehl preemehr/prohxeemoh/oolteemoh...?*
How long does...take? _	¿Cuánto tarda...en llegar? *kwahntoh tahrdah...ehn lyehgahr?*
What time does...arrive_ in...?	¿A qué hora llega...a...? *ah keh ohrah lyegah...ah...?*
Where does the...to... __ leave from?	¿De dónde sale el...a...? *deh dohndeh sahleh ehl...ah...?*
Is this...to...? _____	¿Este es...a...? *ehsteh ehs...ah...?*

6.5 Aeroplanes

● **On arrival** at a Spanish airport, you will find the following signs:

llegadas	salidas
arrivals	departures

6.6 Trains

● **The rail network** is very extensive, run by the RENFE (Red Nacional de Ferrocarriles Españoles). Some local trains are still rather slow so it is preferable to stipulate Talgo or Rápido when buying tickets. During the summer and before public holidays it is advisable to buy train tickets well in advance. Porters are few and far between.

6.7 Taxis

● **There are plenty of taxis** in most cities. Supplements are payable for luggage and travel to stations or airports. It is advisable to inquire about the price in advance and make sure that you are hiring a city taxi.

libre	ocupado	parada de taxis
for hire	booked	taxi rank

Taxi! _____	¡Taxi!
	tahxee!
Could you get me a ___ taxi, please?	¿Me podría llamar un taxi?
	meh pohdreeah lyahmahr oon tahksee?
Where can I find a taxi _ around here?	¿Dónde se puede coger un taxi por aquí?
	dohndeh seh pwehdeh kohhehr oon tahxee pohr ahkee?
Could you take me ____ to..., please?	A..., por favor
	ah..., pohr fahbohr
– this address _____	A esta dirección, por favor
	ah ehstah deerehkthyohn, pohr fahbohr
– the...hotel _____	Al hotel..., por favor
	ahl ohtehl..., pohr fahbohr
– the town/city centre _	Al centro, por favor
	ahl thehntroh, pohr fahbohr
– the station _____	A la estación, por favor
	ah lah ehstahthyohn, pohr fahbohr
– the airport_____	Al aeropuerto, por favor
	ahl ahehrohpwehrtoh, pohr fahbohr
How much is the _____ trip to...?	¿Cuánto sale el recorrido hasta...?
	kwahntoh sahleh ehl rehkohrreedoh ahstah...?
How far is it to...?_____	¿Cuánto es hasta...?
	kwahntoh ehs ahstah...?

Could you turn on the meter, please?	¿Podría poner en marcha el taxímetro?
	pohdreeah pohnehr ehn mahrchah ehl tahxeemehtroh?
I'm in a hurry_____	Llevo prisa
	lyehboh preesah
Could you speed up/slow down a little?	¿Podría ir más rápido/más despacio?
	pohdreeah eer mahs rahpeedoh/mahs dehspathyoh?
Could you take a different route?	¿Podría ir por otro camino?
	pohdreeah eer pohr ohtroh kahmeenoh?
I'd like to get out here, please	Déjeme aquí
	dehhehmeh ahkee
You have to go...here __	Siga...aquí
	seegah...ahkee
You have to go straight on here	Siga todo recto aquí
	seegah tohdoh rehktoh akee
You have to turn left here	Doble a la izquierda aquí
	dohbleh ah lah eethkyehrdah ahkee
You have to turn right here	Doble a la derecha aquí
	dohbleh ah lah dehrehchah ahkee
This is it _____	Es aquí
	ehs ahkee
Could you wait a minute for me, please?	Espéreme un momentito, por favor
	ehspehrehmeh oon mohmehnteetoh, pohr fahbohr

7.1 General 93

7.2 Camping 94

   Camping equipment 96

7.3 Hotel/B&B/apartment/holiday house 99

7.4 Complaints 101

7.5 Departure 103

7.1 General

● **There is great variety** in overnight accommodation in Spain.
It is advisable to book (and send confirmation) in advance.
Hotel: stars indicate the degree of comfort; from five stars, the most luxurious, to one star, very basic. Most hotels offer *pensión completa* (full board) or *media pensión* (half board).
Parador: Mainly, but not always, luxurious hotels in converted castles or palaces in exceptional areas. These are very popular and have to be booked very well in advance, but are well worth the visit. They are under government supervision.
Hostal: Family run businesses for the most part, with one to three stars. They do not always provide breakfast, but are clean and can be very well situated.
Albergue: usually country inns.
Albergue de juventud: restricted to members of the international Youth Hostels Association.
Camping: a list of sites can be found at any Tourist Office.

¿Cuánto tiempo piensa quedarse?	How long will you be staying?
Rellene este formulario, por favor	Fill in this form, please
¿Me permite su pasaporte?	Could I see your passport?
Tiene que pagar una fianza	I'll need a deposit
Tiene que pagar por adelantado	You'll have to pay in advance

My name's...I've made a reservation over the phone/by mail	Me llamo...He reservado una habitación por teléfono/por carta *meh lyahmoh...eh rehsehrbahdoh oonah ahbeetahthyohn pohr tehlehfohnoh/pohr kahrtah*

How much is it per night/week/ month?	¿Cuánto sale por noche/semana/mes?
	kwahntoh sahleh pohr nohcheh/sehmahnah/mehs?
We'll be staying at least...nights/weeks	Pensamos quedarnos al menos...noches/semanas
	pehnsahmohs kehdahrnohs ahl mehnohs...nohchehs/sehmahnahs
We don't know yet	Todavía no lo sabemos exactamente
	tohdahbeeah noh loh sahbehmohs ehxahktahmehnteh
Do you allow pets (cats/dogs)?	¿Están permitidos los animales domésticos (perros/gatos)?
	ehstahn pehrmeeteedohs lohs ahneemahlehs dohmehsteekohs(pehrrohs/gahtohs)?
What time does the gate/door open/close?	¿A qué hora cierran/abren la verja/la puerta de entrada?
	ah keh ohrah thyehrrahn/ahbrehn lah behrhah/lah pwehrtah deh ehntrahdah?
Could you get me a taxi, please?	¿Podría llamar un taxi?
	pohdreeah lyahmahr oon tahxee?
Is there any mail for me?	¿Hay carta para mí?
	ay kahrtah pahrah mee?

7.2 Camping

Where's the manager?	¿Dónde está el encargado?
	dohndeh ehstah ehl ehnkahrgahdoh?
Are we allowed to camp here?	¿Podemos acampar aquí?
	pohdehmohs ahkahmpahr ahkee?
There are...of us and ...tents	Somos...personas y...tiendas
	sohmohs...pehrsohnahs ee...tyehndahs

Puede elegir el sitio usted mismo	You can pick your own site
El sitio se lo asignamos nosotros	You'll be allocated a site
Este es el número de su emplazamiento	This is your site number
Por favor pegue esto en el parabrisas del coche	Stick this on your car, please
No pierda esta tarjeta	Please don't lose this card

Can we pick our _____ own site?	¿Podemos elegir el sitio nosotros mismos?
	pohdehmohs ehlehheer ehl seetyoh nohsohtrohs meesmohs?
Do you have a quiet ___ spot for us?	¿Nos podría dar un sitio tranquilo?
	nohs pohdreeah dahr oon seetyoh trahnkeeloh?
Do you have any other _ sites available?	¿No tiene otro sitio libre?
	noh tyehneh ohtroh seetyoh leebreh?
It's too windy/sunny/ ___ shady here.	Hay mucho viento/mucho sol/mucha sombra
	ay moochoh byehntoh/moochoh sohl/moochah sohmbrah
It's too crowded here __	Hay mucha gente
	ay moochah hehnteh
The ground's too _____ hard/uneven	El suelo es muy duro/muy desigual
	ehl swehloh ehs mwee dooroh/mwee dehseegwahl
Do you have a level ____ spot for the camper/caravan/ folding caravan?	¿Tiene un sitio plano para el autocaravana/la caravana/el remolque tienda?
	tyehneh oon seetyoh plahnoh pahrah ehl ahootohkahrahbahnah/lah kahrahbahnah/ehl rehmohlkeh-tyehndah?

Camping equipment

luggage space	el compartimiento de equipaje	*ehl kohmpahrteemyehntoh de ehkeepahḥeh*
can opener	el abrelatas	*ehl ahbrehlahtahs*
butane gas bottle	la bombona (de gas butano)	*lah bohmbohnah (deh gahs bootahnoh)*
pannier	la ciclobolsa	*lah theeklohbohlsah*
gas cooker	el hornillo de gas	*ehl ohrneelyoh deh gahs*
groundsheet	la lona del suelo	*lah lohnah dehl swehloh*
mallet	el martillo	*ehl mahrteelyoh*
hammock	la hamaca	*lah ahmahkah*
jerry can	el bidón	*ehl beedohn*
campfire	la fogata	*lah fohgahtah*
folding chair	la silla plegable	*lah seelyah plehgahbleh*
insulated picnic box	la nevera portátil/la bolsa nevera	*lah nehbehrah pohrtahteel/ lah bohlsah nehbehrah*
ice pack	el acumulador	*ehl akoomoolahdohr*
compass	la brújula	*lah brooḥoolah*
wick	la mecha	*lah mehchah*
corkscrew	el sacacorchos	*ehl sahkahkohrchohs*
airbed	el colchón neumático	*ehl kohlchohn nehoomahteekoh*
airbed plug	el taponcito de la válvula del colchón	*ehl tahpohntheetoh deh lah bahlboolah dehl kohlchohn*
pump	la bomba neumática	*lah bohmbah nehoomahteekah*
awning	el tejadillo	*ehl tehḥahdeelyoh*

Could we have _____ adjoining sites?	¿Tiene dos plazas juntas?	*tyehneh dohs plahthahs hoontahs?*
Can we park the car ___ next to the tent?	¿Podemos aparcar el coche junto a la tienda?	*pohdehmohs ahpahrkahr ehl kohcheh hoontoh ah lah tyehndah?*

karimat	la esterilla	*lah ehstehreelyah*
pan	la olla	*lah ohlyah*
pan handle	el mango de la olla	*ehl mahngoh deh lah ohlyah*
primus stove	el hornillo de querosén	*ehl ohrneelyoh deh kehrohsehn*
zip	la cremallera	*lah krehmalyehrah*
backpack	la mochila	*lah mohcheelah*
guy rope	el viento	*ehl byehntoh*
sleeping bag	el saco de dormir	*ehl sahkoh deh dohrmeer*
storm lantern	el farol de tormentas	*ehl fahrohl deh tohrmehntahs*
camp bed	el catre (de tijera)	*ehl kahtreh (deh teehehrah)*
table	la mesa	*lah mehsah*
tent	la tienda	*lah tyehndah*
tent peg	la estaca	*lah ehstakah*
tent pole	el palo de tienda	*ehl pahloh deh tyehndah*
vacuum flask	el termo	*ehl tehrmoh*
water bottle	la cantimplora	*lah kahnteemplohrah*
clothes peg	la pinza	*lah peenthah*
clothes line	la cuerda de tender ropa	*lah kwehrdah deh tehndehr rohpah*
windbreak	el paravientos/el paraván	*ehl pahrahbyehntohs/ehl pahrahbahn*
torch	la linterna de bolsillo	*lah leentehrnah deh bohlseelyoh*
pocket knife	la navaja	*lah nahbahhah*

How much is it per ____ person/tent/caravan/car?	¿Cuánto sale por persona/tienda/caravana/coche? *kwahntoh sahleh pohr pehrsohnah/tyehndah/ kahrahbahnah/kohcheh?*

Are there any...? _____	¿Hay...?
	ay...?
– any hot showers? ____	¿Hay duchas con agua caliente?
	ay doochahs kohn ahgwah kahlyehnteh?
– washing machines? __	¿Hay lavadoras?
	ay lahbahdohrahs?
Is there a...on the site? _	¿En este camping hay...?
	ehn ehsteh kahmpeen ay...?
Is there a children's ____ play area on the site?	¿En este camping hay un sitio para que jueguen los niños?
	ehn ehsteh kahmpeen ay oon seetyoh pahrah keh hweghehn lohs neenyohs?
Are there covered_____ cooking facilities on the site?	¿En este camping hay un sitio cubierto para cocinar?
	ehn ehsteh kahmpeen ay oon seetyoh koobyehrtoh pahrah kohtheenahr?
Can I rent a safe here? _	¿Tienen caja fuerte para alquilar?
	tyehnehn kahhah fwehrteh pahrah ahlkeelahr?
Are we allowed to _____ barbecue here?	¿Se pueden hacer barbacoas?
	seh pwehdehn ahtehr bahrbahkohahs?
Are there any power ___ points?	¿Hay tomas de corriente eléctrica?
	ay tohmahs deh kohrryehnteh ehlehktreekah?
Is there drinking water?	¿Hay agua potable?
	ay ahgwah pohtahbleh?
When's the rubbish ____ collected?	¿Cuándo pasan a recoger la basura?
	kwahndoh pahsahn ah rehkohhehr lah bahsoorah?
Do you sell gas bottles _ (butane gas/propane gas)?	¿Venden bombonas de gas (butano/propano)?
	behndehn bohmbohnahs deh gahs(bootahnoh/prohpahnoh)?

7.3 Hotel/B&B/apartment/holiday house

Do you have a _____ single/double room available?	¿Le queda alguna habitación individual/doble? *leh kehdah ahlgoonah ahbeetahthyohn eendeebeedwahl/dohbleh?*
per person/per room ___	por persona/por habitación *pohr pehrsohnah/pohr ahbeetahthyohn*
Does that include_____ breakfast/lunch/ dinner?	¿Incluye desayuno/comida/cena? *eenklooyeh dehsahyoonoh/kohmeedah/thehnah?*
Could we have two ____ adjoining rooms?	¿Nos puede dar dos habitaciones una al lado de la otra? *nohs pwehdeh dahr dohs ahbeetahthyohnehs oonah ahl lahdoh deh lah ohtrah?*
with/without_____ toilet/bath/shower	con/sin lavabo propio/baño propio/ducha propia *kohn/seen lahbahboh prohpyoh/bahnyoh prohpyo/doochah prohpyah?*
(not) facing the street __	que (no) dé a la calle *keh (noh) deh ah lah kahlyeh*
with/without a view ____ of the sea	con/sin vista al mar *kohn/seen beestah ahl mahr*
Is there...in the hotel? __	¿El hotel tiene...? *ehl ohtehl tyehneh...?*

Tiene lavabo y ducha en el mismo piso/en su habitación	You can find the toilet and shower on the same floor/en suite
Por aquí, por favor	This way, please
Su habitación está en el...piso; es la número...	Your room is on the...floor, number...

Is there a lift in the _____ hotel?	¿El hotel tiene ascensor? *ehl ohtehl tyehneh ahsthehnsohr?*
Do you have room _____ service?	¿El hotel tiene servicio de habitación? *ehl ohtehl tyehneh sehrbeethyoh deh ahbeetahthyohn?*
Could I see the room? _	¿Puedo ver la habitación? *pwehdoh behr lah ahbeetahthyohn?*
I'll take this room _____	Me quedo con esta habitación *meh kehdoh kohn ehstah abeetathyohn*
We don't like this one _	Esta no nos gusta *ehstah noh nohs goostah*
Do you have a larger/ _ less expensive room?	¿Tiene una habitación más grande/más barata? *tyehneh oonah ahbeetathyohn mahs grahnde/mahs bahrahtah?*
Could you put in a _____ cot?	¿Puede agregar una cuna? *pwehde ahgrehgahr oonah koonah?*
What time's breakfast? _	¿A qué hora es el desayuno? *ah keh ohrah ehs ehl dehsahyoonoh?*
Where's the dining _____ room?	¿Dónde está el comedor? *dohndeh ehstah ehl kohmehdohr?*
Can I have breakfast _____ in my room?	¿Me pueden traer el desayuno a la habitación? *meh pwehdehn trahehr ehl dehsahyoonoh ah lah ahbeetahthyohn?*
Where's the _____ emergency exit/fire escape?	¿Dónde está la salida de emergencia/la escalera de incendios? *dohndeh ehstah lah sahleedah deh ehmehrhehnthyah/lah ehskahlehrah de eenthehndyohs?*
Where can I park my _____ car (safely)?	¿Dónde hay un sitio (seguro) para aparcar el coche? *dohndeh ay oon seetyoh sehgooroh pahrah ahpahrkahr ehl kohcheh?*
The key to room...,_____ please	La llave de la habitación..., por favor *lah lyahbeh deh lah ahbeetahthyohn..., pohr fahbohr*

Could you put this in ___ the safe, please?	¿Podría dejar esto en la caja fuerte? *pohdreeah dehhahr ehstoh ehn lah cahhah fwehrteh?*
Could you wake me____ at...tomorrow?	¿Me podría despertar mañana a las...? *meh pohdreeah dehspehrtahr mahnyahnah ah lahs...?*
Could you find a_____ babysitter for me?	¿Me podría conseguir una niñera para el bebé? *meh pohdreeah kohnsehgeer oonah neenyehrah pahrah ehl behbeh?*
Could I have an extra ___ blanket?	¿Tendría una manta extra? *tehndreeah oonah mahntah ehxtrah?*
What days do the_____ cleaners come in?	¿Qué días limpian la habitación? *keh deeahs leempyahn lah ahbeetahthyohn?*
When are the sheets/ ___ towels/tea towels changed?	¿Cuándo cambian las sábanas/las toallas/los paños de cocina? *kwahndoh kahmbyahn lahs sahbahnahs/lahs tohahllyahs/lohs pahnyohs deh kohtheenah?*

7.4 Complaints

We can't sleep for _____ the noise	No podemos dormir por el ruido *noh pohdehmohs dohrmeer pohr ehl rweedoh*
Could you turn the_____ radio down, please?	¿Podría bajar el volumen de la radio? *pohdreeah bahhahr ehl vohloomehn deh lah rahdyoh?*
We're out of toilet _____ paper	Se ha acabado el papel higiénico. *seh ah ahkahbahdoh ehl pahpehl eehyehneekoh*
There aren't any.../ _____ there's not enough...	No hay.../no hay suficientes... *noh ay.../noh ay soofeethyehntehs...*

The bed linen's dirty ___	La ropa de cama está sucia
	lah rohpah deh kahmah ehstah soothyah
The room hasn't been __ cleaned.	No han limpiado la habitación
	noh ahn leempyahdoh lah ahbeetahthyohn
The kitchen is not clean	La cocina no está limpia
	lah kohtheenah noh ehstah leempyah
The kitchen utensils are dirty	Los utensilios de cocina están sucios
	lohs ootehnseelyohs deh kohtheenah ehstahn soothyohs
The heater's not _____ working	La calefacción no funciona
	lah kahlehfahkthyohn noh foonthyohnah
There's no (hot)_____ water/electricity	No hay agua (caliente)/electricidad
	noh ay ahgwah(kahlyehnteh)/ehlehktreetheedahdh
...is broken_____	...está estropeado
	...ehstah ehstrohpehahdoh
Could you have that ___ seen to?	¿Podrían hacerlo ver?
	pohdreeahn ahthehrloh behr?
Could I have another ___ room/site?	¿Tendría otra habitación/sitio para la tienda?
	tehndreeah ohtrah abeetahthyohn/seetyoh pahrah lah tyehndah?
The bed creaks terribly _	La cama hace mucho ruido
	lah kahmah ahteh moochoh rweedoh
The bed sags _____	La cama es demasiado blanda
	lah kahmah ehs dehmahsyahdoh blahndah
There are bugs/insects _ in our room	Hay muchos bichos/insectos en nuestra habitación
	ay moochohs beechohs/eensehktohs ehn nwehstrah ahbeetahthyohn
This place is full _____ of mosquitos	Está lleno de mosquitos
	ehstah lyehnoh deh mohskeetohs
– cockroaches _____	Está lleno de cucarachas
	ehstah lyehnoh deh kookahrahchahs

7.5 Departure

See also 8.2 Settling the bill

I'm leaving tomorrow. Could I settle my bill, please?	Mañana me voy. ¿Podría pagar la cuenta ahora? *mahnyahnah meh boy. pohdreeah pahgahr lah kwehntah ahohrah?*
What time should we vacate?	¿A qué hora tenemos que dejar...? *ah keh ohrah tehnehmohs keh dehhahr...?*
Could I have my deposit/passport back, please?	¿Me devuelve la fianza/el pasaporte? *meh dehbwehlbeh lah fyahnthah/ehl pahsahpohrteh?*
We're in a terrible hurry	Llevamos mucha prisa *lyehbahmohs moochah preesah*
Could you forward my mail to this address?	¿Podría enviarme la correspondencia a esta dirección? *pohdreeah ehnbyahrmeh lah kohrrehspohndehnthyah ah ehstah deerehkthyohn?*
Could we leave our luggage here until we leave?	¿Podríamos dejar las maletas aquí hasta que nos marchemos? *pohdreeahmohs dehhahr lahs mahlehtahs ahkee ahstah keh nohs mahrchehmohs?*
Thanks for your hospitality	Muchas gracias por la hospitalidad *moochahs grahthyahs pohr lah ohspeetahleedahd*

Money matters

8.1 Banks 105

8.2 Settling the bill 107

● **In general**, banks are open between 9am and 2pm; they are closed on Saturdays. In large cities some main branches open until 4.30. To exchange currency a passport is required. The sign *cambio* indicates that money can be exchanged.

8.1 Banks

Where can I find a _____ bank/an exchange office around here?	¿Dónde hay un banco/una oficina de cambios por aquí? *dohndeh ay oon bahnkoh/oonah ohfeetheenah deh kahmbyohs pohr ahkee?*
Where can I cash this __ traveller's cheque/giro cheque?	¿Dónde puedo cambiar este cheque de viajero/este cheque postal? *dohndeh pwehdoh kahmbyahr ehsteh chehkeh deh byahhehroh/ehsteh chehkeh pohstahl?*
Can I cash this...here? _	¿Puedo cambiar aquí este...? *pwehdoh kahmbyahr ahkee ehsteh...?*
Can I withdraw money _ on my credit card here?	¿Se puede sacar dinero con una tarjeta de crédito? *seh pwehdeh sahkahr deenehroh kohn oonah tahrhehtah deh krehdeetoh?*
What's the minimum/ __ maximum amount?	¿Cuál es el mínimo/el máximo? *kwahl ehs ehl meeneemoh/ehl mahxeemoh?*
Can I take out less_____ than that?	¿También puedo sacar menos? *tahmbyehn pwehdoh sahkahr mehnohs?*
I've had some money __ transferred here. Has it arrived yet?	He pedido un giro telegráfico. ¿Me ha llegado ya? *eh pehdeedoh oon heeroh tehlehgrahfeekoh. meh ah lyehgahdoh yah?*
These are the details ___ of my bank in the UK	Estos son los datos de mi banco en el Reino Unido *ehstohs sohn lohs dahtohs deh mee bahnkoh ehn ehl reynoh ooneedoh*

Firme aquí	Sign here, please
Tiene que rellenar esto	Fill this out, please
¿Me permite su pasaporte?	Could I see your passport, please?
¿Me permite su carnet de identidad?	Could I see some identification, please?
¿Me permite su tarjeta de la caja postal?	Could I see your girobank card, please?
¿Me permite su tarjeta del banco?	Could I see your bank card, please?

This is my bank/giro ___ number — Este es mi número de cuenta bancaria/de la caja postal
ehsteh ehs mee noomehroh deh kwehntah bahnkahryah/deh lah kahhah pohstahl

I'd like to change _____ some money — Quisiera cambiar dinero
keesyehrah kahmbyahr deenehroh

– pounds into..._____ — Libras esterlinas por...
leebrahs ehstehrleenahs pohr...

– dollars into... _____ — Dólares estadounidenses por...
dohlahrehs ehstahdohooneedehnsehs pohr...

What's the exchange___ rate? — ¿A cuánto está el cambio?
ah kwahntoh ehstah ehl kahmbyoh?

Could you give me_____ some small change with it? — ¿Me podría dar sencillo/cambio?
meh pohdreeah dahr sehntheelyoh/kahmbyoh?

This is not right_____ — Esto está mal *ehstoh ehstah mahl*

| No aceptamos tarjetas de crédito/cheques de viajero/moneda extranjera | We don't accept credit cards/traveller's cheques/foreign currency |

8.2 Settling the bill

Could you put it on my bill?	¿Podría cargarlo a mi cuenta?
	pohdreeah kahrgahrloh ah mee kwehntah?
Does this amount include service?	¿Está incluido el servicio en esta cifra?
	ehstah eenklooeedoh ehl sehrbeethyoh ehn ehstah theefrah?
Can I pay by...?	¿Puedo pagar con...?
	pwehdoh pahgahr kohn...?
Can I pay by credit card?	¿Puedo pagar con tarjeta de crédito?
	pwehdoh pahgahr kohn tahrhehtah deh krehdeetoh?
Can I pay by traveller's cheque?	¿Puedo pagar con un cheque de viajero?
	pwehdoh pahgahr kohn oon chehkeh de byahhehroh?
Can I pay with foreign currency?	¿Puedo pagar con moneda extranjera?
	pwehdoh pahgahr kohn mohnehdah ehxtrahnhehrah?
You've given me too much/you haven't given me enough change	Me ha devuelto de más/de menos
	meh ah dehbwehltoh deh mahs/deh mehnohs
Could you check the bill again, please?	¿Puede volver a hacer la cuenta?
	pwehdeh bohlbehr ah ahthehr lah kwehntah?
Could I have a receipt, please?	¿Podría darme un recibo?
	pohdreeah dahrmeh oon rehtheeboh?
I don't have enough money on me	No me alcanza el dinero
	noh meh ahlkahnthah ehl deenehroh
This is for you	Tenga, esto es para usted
	tehngah, ehstoh ehs pahrah oostehdh
Keep the change	Quédese con la vuelta
	kehdehseh kohn lah bwehltah

9
Post and telephone

9.1 Post 109

9.2 Telephone 111

9.1 Post

For giros, see 8 Money matters

● **Post offices** are open from Monday to Saturday from 9am to 1 or 1.30pm. However stamps (*sellos*) can be bought at any *estanco* and many hotels also provide stamps. It is advisable to post letters at a post office, rather than the yellow mail boxes (*buzón*).

giros postales	telegramas	sellos
money orders	telegrams	stamps
paquetes		
parcels		

Where's...?_____	¿Dónde está...?
	dohndeh ehstah...?
Where's the post _____ office?	¿Dónde hay una oficina de Correos por aquí?
	dohndeh ay oonah ohfeetheenah deh kohrrehohs pohr ahkee?
Where's the main post _ office?	¿Dónde está la oficina central de Correos?
	dohndeh ehstah lah ohfeetheenah thehntrahl deh kohrrehohs?
Where's the postbox? __	¿Dónde hay un buzón por aquí?
	dohndeh ahee oon boothohn pohr ahkee?
Which counter should __ I go to...?	¿Cuál es la ventanilla para...?
	kwahl ehs lah behntahneelyah pahrah...?
– to send a fax _____	¿Cuál es la ventanilla para enviar un fax?
	kwahl ehs lah behntahneelyah pahrah ehnbyahr oon fahx?

– to change money _____	¿Cuál es la ventanilla para cambiar dinero?
	kwahl ehs lah behntahneelyah pahrah kahmbyahr deenehroh?
– to change giro _____ cheques	¿Cuál es la ventanilla para los cheques postales?
	kwahl ehs lah behntahneelyah pahrah lohs chehkehs pohstahlehs?
– for a Telegraph _____ Money Order?	¿Cuál es la ventanilla para los giros telegráficos?
	kwahl ehs lah behntahneelyah pahrah lohs <u>h</u>eerohs tehlehgrahfeekohs?
Poste restante _____	Lista de correos
	leestah deh kohrrehohs
Is there any mail _____ for me? My name's...	¿Hay carta para mí? Me llamo...
	ay kahrtah pahrah mee? meh lyahmoh...

Stamps

What's the postage _____ for a...to...?	¿Cuánto se le pone a un(a)...para...?
	kwahntoh seh leh pohneh ah oon(ah)...pahrah...?
Are there enough _____ stamps on it?	¿Lleva suficiente franqueo?
	lyehbah soofeethyehnteh frahnkehoh?
I'd like... ...euro_____ stamps	Déme...sellos de...
	dehmeh...sehlyohs deh...
I'd like to send this... ____	Quisiera enviar esto...
	keesyehrah ehnbyahr ehstoh...
– express _____	Quisiera enviar esto por correo urgente
	keesyehrah ehnbyahr ehstoh pohr kohrrehoh oor<u>h</u>ehnteh
– by air mail_____	Quisiera enviar esto por avión
	keesyehrah ehnbyahr ehstoh pohr ahbyohn
– by registered mail ____	Quisiera enviar esto certificado
	keesyehrah ehnbyahr ehstoh thehrteefeekahdoh

Telegram/fax

I'd like to send a_____ telegram to...	Quisiera mandar un telegrama a... *keesyehrah mahndahr oon tehlehgrahmah ah...*
How much is that_____ per word?	¿Cuánto cuesta por palabra? *kwahntoh kwehstah pohr pahlahbrah?*
This is the text I want __ to send	Este es el texto que quiero enviar *ehsteh ehs ehl tehxtoh keh kyehroh ehnbyahr*
Shall I fill in the form ___ myself?	¿Relleno yo mismo el formulario? *rehlyehnoh yoh meesmoh ehl fohrmoolahryoh?*
Can I make _____ photocopies/ send a fax here?	¿Se pueden hacer fotocopias/se puede enviar un fax aquí? *seh pwehdehn ahthehr fohtohkohpyahs/seh pwehdeh ehnbyahr oon fahx ahkee?*
How much is it _____ per page?	¿Cuánto cuesta por página? *kwahntoh kwehstah pohr pahheenah?*

9.2 Telephone

See also 1.8 Telephone alphabet

● **All phone booths** offer a direct international service to the UK or US (07 - country code 44 (UK) or 1 (US) – trunk code minus 0 – number). Area codes are displayed. It is easier, and may even be cheaper to place your call from the *Telefónica* or telephone office. When phoning someone in Spain, you will not be greeted with the subscriber's name but diga or *dígame*.

Is there a phone box ___ around here?	¿Hay alguna cabina teléfonica por aquí? *ay ahlgoonah kahbeenah tehlehfohneekah pohr ahkee?*

Could I use your_____ phone, please?	¿Podría usar su teléfono?
	pohdreeah oosahr soo tehlehfohnoh?
Do you have a _____ (city/region)...phone directory?	¿Tiene una guía de teléfonos de la ciudad/la provincia de...?
	tyehneh oonah gheeah deh tehlehfohnohs deh lah thyoodahdh/lah prohbeenthyah deh...?
Where can I get a_____ phone card?	¿Dónde puedo conseguir una tarjeta de teléfonos?
	dohndeh pwehdoh kohnsehgheer oonah tahrhehtah deh tehlehfohnohs?
Could you give me...? __	¿Me podría dar...?
	meh pohdreeah dahr...?
– the number for_____ international directory enquiries	¿Me podría dar el número de información internacional?
	meh pohdreeah dahr ehl noomehroh deh eenfohrmahthyohn eentehrnahthyohnahl?
– the number of room...	¿Me podría dar el número de la habitación...?
	meh pohdreeah dahr ehl noomehroh deh lah ahbeetahthyohn...?
– the international _____ access code	¿Me podría dar el indicativo internacional?
	meh pohdreeah dahr ehl eendeekahteeboh eentehrnahthyonahl...?
– the country code_____ for...	¿Me podría dar el indicativo de...?
	meh pohdreeah dahr ehl eendeekahteeboh deh...?
– the trunk code for... __	¿Me podría dar el prefijo de...?
	meh pohdreeah dahr ehl prehfeehoh deh...?
– the number of..._____	¿Me podría dar el número de abonado de...?
	meh pohdreeah dahr ehl noomehroh deh ahbohnahdoh deh...?

Could you check if this number's correct?	¿Podría controlar si está bien este número?
	pohdreeah kohntrohlahr see ehstah byehn ehsteh noomehroh?
Can I dial international direct?	¿Se puede llamar directamente al extranjero?
	seh pwehdeh lyahmahr deerehktahmehnteh ahl ehxtrahnhehroh?
Do I have to go through the switchboard?	¿Hay que llamar por operadora?
	ay keh lyahmahr pohr ohpehrahdohrah?
Do I have to dial '0' first?	¿Hay que marcar primero el cero?
	ay keh mahrkahr preemehroh ehl thehroh?
Do I have to book my calls?	¿Hay que pedir línea?
	ay keh pehdeer leenehah?
Could you dial this number for me, please?	¿Podría usted llamar a este número?
	pohdreeah oostehdh lyahmahr ah ehsteh noomehroh?
Could you put me through to.../extension..., please?	¿Me podría poner con.../con la extensión...?
	meh pohdreeah pohnehr kohn.../kohn lah ehxtehnsyohn...?
I'd like to place a reverse-charge call to...	Quisiera una llamada de cobro revertido a...
	keesyehrah oonah lyahmahdah deh kohbroh rehbehrteedoh ah...
What's the charge per minute?	¿Cuánto cuesta por minuto?
	kwahntoh kwehstah pohr meenootoh?
Have there been any calls for me?	¿Ha habido alguna llamada para mí?
	ah ahbeedoh ahlgoonah lyahmahdah pahrah mee?

The conversation

Hello, this is... _____	Buenos días, soy...
	bwehnohs deeahs, soy...
Who is this, please? ___	¿Con quién hablo?
	kohn kyehn ahbloh?
Is this...? _____	¿Hablo con...?
	ahbloh kohn...?
I'm sorry, I've dialled ___ the wrong number	Perdone, me he equivocado de número
	pehrdohneh, meh eh ehkeebohkahdoh deh noomehroh
I can't hear you_____	No le oigo bien
	noh leh oygoh byehn
I'd like to speak to... ___	Quisiera hablar con...
	keesyehrah ahblahr kohn...
Is there anybody_____ who speaks English?	¿Hay alguien que hable inglés?
	ay ahlghyehn keh ahbleh eenglehs?

Lo llaman por teléfono	There's a phone call for you
Primero tiene que marcar el cero	You have to dial '0' first
Un momento, por favor	One moment, please
No contestan	There's no answer
Está comunicando	The line's engaged
¿Quiere esperar?	Do you want to hold?
Ahora le paso	Putting you through
Se ha equivocado de número	You've got a wrong number
El señor/la señora...no está en estos momentos.	He's/she's not here right now
El señor/la señora...no estará hasta...	He'll/she'll be back...
Este es el contestador automático de...	This is the answering machine of...

Extension..., please	¿Me pone con la extensión...?
	meh pohneh kohn lah ehxtehnsyohn...?
Could you ask him/her to call me back?	¿Podría decirle que me llame?
	pohdreeah dehtheerleh keh meh lyahmeh?
My name's... My number's...	Me llamo...Mi número es...
	meh lyahmoh...mee noomehroh ehs...
Could you tell him/her I called?	¿Puede decirle que he llamado?
	pwehdeh dehtheerleh keh eh lyahmahdoh?
I'll call back tomorrow	Lo/la volveré a llamar mañana
	loh/lah bohlbehreh ah lyahmahr mahnyahnah

10
Shopping

10.1 Shopping conversations 117

10.2 Food 120

10.3 Clothing and shoes 121

10.4 Photographs and video 123

10.5 At the hairdresser's 125

● **Opening times:** Mon–Fri, 9.30–1.30 and 5–8. Department stores are open in the afternoons from 4pm and remain open on Saturdays. Other shops generally close on Saturdays at 1pm. In tourist areas shops open for longer periods. Chemists display the list of *farmacias de guardia* (those open on Sundays and after hours).

10.1 Shopping conversations

Where can I get...?	¿Dónde puedo conseguir...?
	dohndeh pwehdoh kohnsehgheer...?
When does this shop open?	¿De qué hora a qué hora abren?
	deh keh ohrah ah keh ohrah ahbrehn?
Could you tell me where the...department is?	¿Me podría indicar la sección de...?
	meh pohdreeah eendeekahr lah sehkthyohn deh...?
Could you help me, please? I'm looking for...	¿Podría ayudarme? Busco...
	pohdreeah ahyoodahrmeh? booskoh...
Do you sell British/ American newspapers?	¿Venden periódicos británicos/americanos?
	behndehn pehryohdeekohs breetahneekohs/ahmehreekahnohs?

¿Lo/la atienden?	Are you being served?

No, I'd like...	No. Quisiera...
	noh. keesyehrah...
I'm just looking, if that's all right	Sólo estoy mirando, gracias
	sohloh ehstoy meerahndoh, grahthyahs

¿Algo más?	Anything else?

almacén
department store

antigüedades
antiques

artículos de deporte
sports shop

artículos del hogar
household goods

artículos dietéticos
health food shop

artículos fotográficos
camera shop

artículos usados
second hand goods

autoservicio
self service

bicicletas
bicycle shop

bodega
off licence

bricolaje
DIY-store

carnicería
butcher's shop

casa de música
music shop

centro comercial
shopping centre

comestibles
grocery store

decoración (de interiores)
interior design shop

droguería
household products and cosmetics

electrodomésticos
electrical appliances

estanco
tobacconist

farmacia
chemist

ferretería
hardware shop

floristería
florist

frutas y verduras
greengrocer

galería comercial
shopping arcade

heladería
ice cream parlour

joyería
jeweller

juguetería
toy shop

lavandería
laundry

lechería
dairy

librería
book shop

mercado
market

mercería
draper

óptica
optician

panadería
bakery

pastelería
cake shop

peluquería (señoras, caballeros)
hairdresser

perfumería
cosmetics

pescadería
fishmonger

quiosco
news stand

recuerdos de viaje
souvenir shop

reparación de bicicletas
bicycle repair shop

revistas y prensa
newsagent

salón de belleza
beauty parlour

supermercado
supermarket

tienda
shop

tienda de modas
clothes shop

tintorería
drycleaner

zapatería
shoe shop

zapatero
cobbler

Yes, I'd also like... _____	Sí, también déme...
	see, tahmbyehn dehmeh...
No, thank you. That's __ all	No, gracias. Es todo
	noh, grahthyahs, ehs tohdoh
Could you show me...? _	¿Me podría mostrar...?
	meh pohdreeah mohstrahr...?
I'd prefer... _____	Prefiero...
	prehfyehroh...
This is not what I'm ____ looking for	No es lo que busco
	noh ehs loh keh booskoh
Thank you. I'll keep ____ looking	Gracias. Voy a seguir mirando
	grahthyahs. boy ah sehgheer meerahndoh
Do you have _____ something...?	¿No tendría algo ...?
	noh tehndreeah ahlgoh ...?
– less expensive?_____	¿No tendría algo más barato?
	noh tehndreeah ahlgoh mahs bahrahtoh?
– smaller? _____	¿No tendría algo más pequeño?
	noh tehndreeah ahlgoh mahs pehkehnyoh?
– larger?_____	¿No tendría algo más grande?
	noh tehndreeah ahlgoh mahs grahndeh?
I'll take this one _____	Me llevo éste/ésta
	meh lyehboh ehsteh/ehstah

Lo siento; no lo tenemos	I'm sorry, we don't have that
Lo siento; ya no queda	I'm sorry, we're sold out
Lo siento, hasta el...no lo tendremos	I'm sorry, that won't be in until...
Pague en la caja, por favor	You can pay at the cash desk
No aceptamos tarjetas de crédito	We don't accept credit cards
No aceptamos cheques de viajero	We don't accept traveller's cheques
No aceptamos moneda extranjera	We don't accept foreign currency

Does it come with _____ instructions?	¿Viene con instrucciones? *byehneh kohn eenstrookthyohnehs?*
It's too expensive _____	Me parece muy caro *meh pahrehtheh mwee kahroh*
I'll give you... _____	Le doy... *leh doy...*
Could you keep _____ this for me? I'll come back for it later	¿Me lo/la podría guardar? Volveré más tarde a buscarlo *meh loh/lah pohdreeah gwahrdahr? bohlbehreh mahs tahrdeh ah booskahrloh*
Have you got a bag _____ for me, please?	¿Tendría una bolsita? *tehndreeah oonah bohlseetah?*
Could you giftwrap _____ it, please?	¿Me lo podría envolver para regalo? *meh loh pohdreeah ehnbohlbehr pahrah rehgahloh?*

10.2 Food

I'd like a hundred _____ grams of..., please	Quisiera cien gramos de... *keesyehrah thyehn grahmohs deh...*
– half a kilo of... _____	Quisiera medio kilo de... *keesyehrah mehdyoh keeloh deh...*
– a kilo of... _____	Quisiera un kilo de... *keesyehrah oon keeloh deh...*
Could you...it for me, _____ please?	¿Me lo podría...? *meh loh pohdreeah...?*
Could you slice it/ _____ dice it for me, please?	¿Me lo podría cortar en lonchas/en trozos? *meh loh pohdreeah kohrtahr ehn lohnchahs/ehn trohthohs?*
Could you grate it _____ for me, please?	¿Me lo podría rallar? *meh loh pohdreeah rahlyahr?*
Can I order it? _____	¿Se lo podría encargar? *seh loh pohdreeah ehnkahrgahr?*
I'll pick it up tomorrow/ _____ at...	Pasaré a buscarlo mañana/a las... *pahsahreh ah booskahrloh mahnyahnah/ah lahs...*

Can you eat/drink this? _	¿Es para comer/beber?
	ehs pahrah kohmehr/behbehr?
What's in it? _____	¿Qué lleva dentro?
	keh lyehbah dehntroh?

10.3 Clothing and shoes

I saw something in the _ window. Shall I point it out?	He visto algo en el escaparate. ¿Se lo enseño?
	eh beestoh ahlgoh ehn ehl ehskahpahrahteh, seh loh ehnsehnyoh?
I'd like something to ___ go with this	Busco algo que haga juego con esto
	booskoh ahlgoh keh ahgah hwehgoh kohn ehstoh
Do you have shoes ____ in this colour?	¿Tiene zapatos de este color?
	tyehneh thahpahtohs deh ehsteh kohlohr?
I'm a size...in the UK ___	En el Reino Unido tengo el número...
	ehn ehl reheenoh ooneedoh tehngoh ehl noomehroh...
Can I try this on? _____	¿Me lo podría probar?
	meh loh pohdreeah prohbahr?
Where's the fitting _____ room?	¿Dónde está el probador?
	dohndeh ehstah ehl prohbahdohr?
It doesn't fit_____	No me vale
	noh meh bahleh
This is the right size____	Este es mi número
	ehsteh ehs mee noomehroh
It doesn't suit me _____	No me está bien
	noh meh ehstah byehn
Do you have this/_____ these in...?	¿Tiene éste/ésta, pero en...?
	tyehneh ehsteh/ehstah pehroh ehn...?
The heel's too high/low_	El tacón me parece muy alto/bajo
	ehl tahkohn meh pahrehtheh mwee ahltoh/bahhoh
Is this/are these _____ genuine leather?	¿Es/son de piel auténtica?
	ehs/sohn deh pyehl ah-ootehnteekah?

No planchar	Colgar mojado	Lavado a mano
Do not iron	Drip dry	Hand wash
No centrifugar	Lavado en seco	Lavado a máquina
Do not spin dry	Dry clean	Machine wash

I'm looking for a... _____ for a...-year-old baby/child	Busco un/una...para un bebé/niño de...años *booskoh oon/oonah...pahrah oon behbeh/neenyoh deh...ahnyohs*
I'd like a... ... _____	Quisiera un/una...de... *keesyehrah oon/oonah...deh...*
– silk _____	Quisiera un/una...de seda *keesyehrah oon/oonah...deh sehdah*
– cotton _____	Quisiera un/una...de algodón *keesyehrah oon/oonah...deh ahlgohdohn*
– woollen _____	Quisiera un/una...de lana *keesyehrah oon/oonah...deh lahnah*
– linen_____	Quisiera un/una...de hilo *keesyehrah oon/oonah...deh eeloh*
What temperature _____ can I wash it at?	¿A qué temperatura lo puedo lavar? *ah keh tehmpehrahtoorah loh pwehdoh lahbahr?*
Will it shrink in the _____ wash?	¿Encoge al lavarlo? *enkoh<u>h</u>eh ahl lahbahrloh?*

At the cobbler

Could you mend_____ these shoes?	¿Podría arreglar estos zapatos? *pohdreeah ahrrehglahr ehstohs thahpahtohs?*
Could you put new ____ soles/heels on these?	¿Podría ponerle nuevas suelas/nuevos tacones? *pohdreeah pohnehrleh nwehbahs swehlahs/nwehbohs tahkohnehs?*
When will they be_____ ready?	¿Para cuándo van a estar? *pahrah kwahndoh bahn ah ehstahr?*

I'd like..., please _____	Quisiera..., por favor
	keesyehrah..., pohr fahbohr
– a tin of shoe polish ___	Quisiera una crema para zapatos
	keesyehrah oonah krehmah pahrah thahpahtohs
– a pair of shoelaces ___	Quisiera un par de cordones
	keesyehrah oon pahr deh kohrdohnehs

10.4 Photographs and video

I'd like a film for this ___ camera, please	Quisiera un rollo/carrete para esta cámara
	keesyehrah oon rohlyoh/kahrrehteh pahrah ehstah kahmahrah
– a 126 cartridge _____	Quisiera una película en cassette de 126
	keesyehrah oonah pehleekoolah ehn kahseht deh thyehntoh beheenteesehees
– a 35mm colour slide__	Un carrete de 35mm para diapositivas en color
	oon kahrrehteh deh treyntah ee theenkoh meeleemehtrohs pahrah deeapohseeteebahs ehn kohlohr
– a 35mm colour _____ print	Un carrete de 35mm en color
	oon kahrrehteh deh treyntah ee theenkoh meeleemehtrohs ehn kohlohr
– a 35mm black _____ and white	Un carrete de 35mm en blanco y negro
	oon kahrrehteh deh treyntah ee theenkoh meeleemehtrohs ehn blahnkoh ee nehgroh
– a videotape _____	Quisiera una cinta de vídeo
	keesyehrah oonah theentah deh veedehoh
colour/black and white _	color/blanco y negro
	kohlohr/blahnkoh ee nehgroh
super eight _____	superocho
	soopehrohchoh

12/24/36 exposures_____	doce/veinticuatro/treinta y seis fotos
	dohtheh/beheenteekwahtroh/treheentah ee sehees fohtohs
ASA/DIN number _____	valor ISO
	bahlohr eesoh
daylight film_____	película para luz natural
	pehleekoolah pahrah looth nahtoorahl
film for artificial light ___	película para luz artificial
	pehleekoolah pahrah looth ahrteefeethyah

Problems

Could you load the _____ film for me, please?	¿Me podría poner el rollo/carrete en la cámara?
	meh pohdreeah pohnehr ehl rohlyoh/kahrrehteh ehn lah kahmahrah?
Could you take the film_ out for me, please?	¿Me podría sacar el rollo/carrete de la cámara?
	meh pohdreeah sahkahr ehl rohlyoh/kahrrehteh deh lah kahmahrah?
Should I replace _____ the batteries?	¿Tengo que cambiar las pilas?
	tehngoh keh kahmbyahr lahs peelahs?
Could you have a look _ at my camera, please? It's not working	¿Me podría revisar la cámara? Ya no funciona
	meh pohdreeah rehbeesahr lah kahmahrah? yah noh foonthyohnah
The...is broken _____	Está estropeado el...
	ehstah ehstrohpehahdoh ehl...
The film's jammed _____	Se ha atascado el rollo/carrete
	seh ah ahtahskahdoh ehl rohlyoh/kahrrehteh
The film's broken _____	Se ha roto el rollo/carrete
	seh ah rohtoh ehl rohlyoh/kahrrehteh
The flash isn't working _	No funciona el flash
	noh foonthyohnah ehl flahsh

Processing and prints

I'd like to have this film developed/printed, please	Quisiera mandar a revelar/copiar este rollo/carrete
	keesyehrah mahndahr ah rehbehlahr/kohpyahr ehsteh rohlyoh/kahrrehteh
I'd like...prints from ____ each negative	Quisiera...copias de cada negativo
	keesyehrah...kohpyahs deh kahdah nehgahteeboh
glossy/mat_____	brillante/mate
	breelyahnte/mahteh
I'd like to reorder _____ these photos	Quisiera encargar más copias de estas fotos
	keesyehrah ehnkahrgahr mahs kohpyahs deh ehstahs fohtohs
I'd like to have this____ photo enlarged	Quisiera una ampliación de esta foto
	keesyehrah oonah ahmplyahthyohn deh ehstah fohtoh
How much is_____ processing?	¿Cuánto sale el revelado?
	kwahntoh sahleh ehl rehbehlahdoh?
– printing? _____	¿Cuánto sale el copiado?
	kwahntoh sahleh ehl kohpyahdoh?
– extra copies?_____	¿Cuánto salen las copias adicionales?
	kwahntoh sahlehn lahs kohpyahs ahdeethyohnahlehs?
– the enlargement? ____	¿Cuánto sale la ampliación?
	kwahntoh sahleh lah ahmplyahthyohn?
When will they _____ be ready?	¿Para cuándo van a estar?
	pahrah kwahndoh bahn ah ehstahr?

10.5 At the hairdresser's

Do I have to make an ___ appointment?	¿Tengo que pedir hora?
	tehngoh keh pehdeer ohrah?

Can I come in straight away?	¿Podría atenderme en seguida?
	pohdreeah ahtehndehrmeh ehn sehgheedah?
How long will I have to wait?	¿Cuánto tengo que esperar?
	kwahntoh tehngoh keh ehspehrahr?
I'd like a shampoo/haircut	Quisiera lavarme/cortarme el pelo
	keesyehrah lahbahrmeh/kohrtahrmeh ehl pehloh
I'd like a shampoo for oily/dry hair, please	Quisiera un champú para cabello graso/seco
	keesyehrah oon chahmpoo pahrah kahbehlyoh grahsoh/sehkoh
an anti-dandruff shampoo	Quisiera un champú anticaspa
	keesyehrah oon chahmpoo ahnteekahspah
– a shampoo for permed/coloured hair	Quisiera un champú para cabello con permanente/teñido.
	keesyehrah oon chahmpoo pahrah kahbehlyoh kohn pehrmahnehnteh/tehnyeedoh
– a colour rinse shampoo	Quisiera un champú color
	keesyehrah oon chahmpoo kohlohr
– a shampoo with conditioner	Quisiera un champú con acondicionador
	keesyehrah oon chahmpoo kohn ahkohndeethyohnahdohr
– highlights	Quisiera que me hagan claritos
	keesyehrah keh meh ahgahn klahreetohs
Do you have a colour chart, please?	¿Tendría una carta de colores?
	tehndreeah oonah kahrtah deh kohlohrehs?
I want to keep it the same colour	Quiero conservar el mismo color
	kyehroh kohnsehrbahr ehl meesmoh kohlohr
I'd like it darker/lighter	Quisiera un color más oscuro/más claro
	keesyehrah oon kohlohr mahs ohskooroh/mahs klahroh
I'd like/I don't want hairspray	(No) quiero fijador
	(noh) kyehroh fee<u>h</u>ahdohr

– gel _____	(No) quiero gel *(noh) kyehroh <u>h</u>ehl*
– lotion _____	(No) quiero loción *(noh) kyehroh lohthyohn*
I'd like a short fringe ___	Quisiera el flequillo corto *keesyehrah ehl flehkeelyoh kohrtoh*
Not too short at _____ the back	No lo quisiera demasiado corto por detrás *noh loh keesyehrah dehmahsyahdoh* *kohrtoh pohr dehtrahs*
Not too long here_____	No lo quisiera demasiado largo aquí *noh loh keesyehrah dehmahsyahdoh* *lahrgoh ahkee*
I'd like/I don't want ____ (many) curls	(No) quisiera (demasiados) rizos *(noh) keesyehrah (dehmahsyadohs)* *reethohs*
It needs a little/_____ a lot taken off	Hay que cortar sólo un trocito/un buen trozo *ay keh kohrtahr sohloh oon* *trohtheetoh/oon bwehn trohthoh*
I want a completely ____ different style	Quisiera un modelo totalmente diferente *keesyehrah oon mohdehloh* *tohtahlmehnteh deefehrehnteh*
I'd like it the same as..._	Quisiera el pelo como... *keesyehrah ehl pehloh kohmoh...*
– as that lady's _____	Quisiera el pelo como esa señora *keesyehrah ehl pehloh kohmoh ehsah* *sehnyohrah*
– as in this photo _____	Quisiera el pelo como en esta foto *keesyehrah ehl pehloh kohmoh ehn ehstah* *fohtoh*
Could you put the _____ drier up/down a bit?	¿Podría poner el casco más alto/bajo? *pohdreeah pohnehr ehl kahskoh mahs* *ahltoh/ bah<u>h</u>oh?*
I'd like a facial_____	Quisiera una máscara facial *keesyehrah oonah mahskahrah fahthyahl*

– a manicure _____	Quisiera que me hagan manicura *keesyehrah keh meh ahgahn* *mahneekoorah*
– a massage _____	Quisiera que me hagan masaje *keesyehrah keh meh ahgahn mahsahheh*
Could you trim _____ my fringe?	¿Me podría recortar el flequillo? *meh pohdreeah rehkohrtahr ehl* *flehkeelyoh?*
– my beard? _____	¿Me podría recortar la barba? *meh pohdreeah rehkohrtahr lah bahrbah?*
– my moustache? _____	¿Me podría recortar el bigote? *meh pohdreeah rehkohrtahr ehl* *beegohteh?*
I'd like a shave, please _	Aféiteme, por favor *ahfeheetehmeh, pohr fahbohr*
I'd like a wet shave, _____ please	Aféiteme a navaja, por favor *ahfeheetehmeh ah nahbahhah, pohr* *fahbohr*

¿Cómo quiere el corte de pelo?	How do you want it cut?
¿Qué modelo deseaba?	What style did you have in mind?
¿Qué color quiere?	What colour do you want it?
¿Esta temperatura le va bien?	Is the temperature all right for you?
¿Quiere algo para leer?	Would you like something to read?
¿Quiere algo para beber?	Would you like a drink?
¿Así está bien?	Is this what you had in mind?

11

At the Tourist Information Centre

11.1 Places of interest 130

11.2 Going out 133

11.3 Booking tickets 135

11.1 Places of interest

Where's the Tourist Information, please?	¿Dónde está la oficina de turismo?
	dohndeh ehstah lah ohfeetheenah deh tooreesmoh?
Do you have a city map?	¿Tendría un plano de la ciudad?
	tehndreeah oon plahnoh deh lah thyoodahdh?
Where is the museum?	¿Dónde está el museo?
	dohndeh ehstah ehl moosehoh?
Where can I find a church?	¿Dónde podría encontrar una iglesia?
	dohndeh pohdreeah ehnkohntrahr oonah eeglehsyah?
Could you give me some information about...?	¿Me podría dar información sobre...?
	meh pohdreeah dahr eenfohrmahthyohn sohbreh...?
How much is that?	¿Cuánto le debemos por esto?
	kwahntoh leh dehbehmohs pohr ehstoh?
What are the main places of interest?	¿Cuáles son los sitios más interesantes para visitar?
	kwahlehs sohn lohs seetyohs mahs eentehrehsahntehs pahrah veeseetahr?
Could you point them out on the map?	¿Me los podría señalar en el plano?
	meh lohs pohdreeah sehnyahlahr ehn ehl plahnoh?
What do you recommend?	¿Qué nos recomienda?
	keh nohs rehkohmyehndah?
We'll be here for a few hours	Pensamos quedarnos unas horas
	pehnsahmohs kehdahrnohs oonahs ohrahs
– a day	Pensamos quedarnos un día
	pehnsahmohs kehdahrnohs oon deeah
– a week	Pensamos quedarnos una semana
	pehnsahmohs kehdahrnohs oonah sehmahnah
We're interested in...	Nos interesa...
	nohs eentehrehsah...

Is there a scenic walk around the city?	¿Hay algún circuito turístico para visitar la ciudad a pie?
	ay ahlgoon theerkweetoh tooreesteekoh pahrah veeseetar lah thyoodahdh ah pyeh?
How long does it take?	¿Cuánto dura?
	kwahntoh doorah?
Where does it start/end?	¿De dónde sale?/¿Dónde termina?
	deh dohndeh sahleh?/dohndeh tehrmeenah?
Are there any boat cruises here?	¿Hay excursiones en barco?
	ay ehxkoorsyohnehs ehn bahrkoh?
Where can we board?	¿Dónde se puede embarcar?
	dohndeh seh pwehdeh ehmbahrkahr?
Are there any bus tours?	¿Hay excursiones en autocar?
	ay ehxkoorsyohnehs ehn ahootohkahr?
Where do we get on?	¿De dónde salen?
	deh dohndeh sahlehn?
Is there a guide who speaks English?	¿Hay algún guía que hable inglés?
	ay ahlgoon gheeah keh ahbleh eenglehs?
What trips can we take around the area?	¿Qué excursiones se pueden hacer en los alrededores?
	keh ehxkoorsyohnehs seh pwehdehn ahthehr ehn lohs ahlrehdehdohrehs?
Are there any excursions?	¿Hay excursiones organizadas?
	ay ehxkoorsyohnehs ohrgahneethahdahs?
Where do they go to?	¿Hacia dónde van?
	ahthyah dohndeh bahn?
We'd like to go to...	Quisiéramos ir a...
	keesyehrahmohs eer ah...
How long is the trip?	¿Cuánto se tarda en llegar?
	kwahntoh seh tahrdah ehn lyehgahr?
How long do we stay in...?	¿Cuánto dura la visita a...?
	kwahntoh doorah lah beeseetah ah...
Are there any guided tours?	¿Hay visitas guiadas?
	ay beeseetahs gheeahdahs?

How much free time will we have there?	¿Cuánto tiempo libre tenemos allí? *kwahntoh tyehmpoh leebreh tehnehmohs alyee?*
We want to go hiking	Nos gustaría hacer una excursión a pie *nohs goostahreeah ahthehr oonah ehxkoorsyohn ah pyeh*
Can we hire a guide?	¿Es posible contratar un guía? *ehs pohseebleh kohntrahtahr oon gheeah?*
Can I book mountain huts?	¿Se puede hacer una reserva para un refugio (en la montaña)? *seh pwehdeh ahthehr oonah rehsehrbah pahrah oon rehfoohyoh (ehn lah mohntahnyah)?*
What time does... open/close?	¿A qué hora abre/cierra...? *ah keh ohrah ahbreh/thyehrrah...?*
What days is...open/ closed?	¿Qué días tiene abierto/cerrado...? *keh deeahs tyehneh ahbyehrtoh/thehrrahdoh...?*
What's the admission price?	¿Cuánto sale la entrada? *kwahntoh sahleh lah ehntrahdah?*
Is there a group discount?	¿Hay descuento para grupos? *ay dehskwehntoh pahrah groopohs?*
Is there a child discount?	¿Hay descuento para niños? *ay dehskwehntoh pahrah neenyohs?*
Is there a discount for pensioners?	¿Hay descuento para jubilados? *ay dehskwehntoh pahrah hoobeelahdohs?*
Can I take (flash) photos/can I film here?	¿Se pueden sacar fotos (con flash)/ filmar aquí? *seh pwehdehn sahkahr fohtohs(kohn flahsh)/feelmahr ahkee?*
Do you have any postcards of...?	¿Venden postales de...? *behndehn pohstahlehs deh...?*
Do you have an English...?	¿Tiene un...en inglés? *tyehneh oon...ehn eenglehs?*
– an English catalogue?	¿Tiene un catálogo en inglés? *tyehneh oon kahtahlohgoh ehn eenglehs?*

| – an English_____ programme? | ¿Tiene un programa en inglés? *tyehneh oon prohgrahmah ehn eenglehs?* |
| – an English brochure? _ | ¿Tiene un folleto en inglés? *tyehneh oon fohlyehtoh ehn eenglehs?* |

11.2 Going out

● **At the cinema** most films are dubbed in Spanish. Sometimes there are only two showings, in the evening, at 7 and 11pm. In this case advance booking is advisable.

Do you have this _____ week's/month's entertainment guide?	¿Tiene la guía de los espectáculos de esta semana/este mes? *tyehneh lah gheeah deh lohs ehspehktahkoolohs deh ehstah sehmahnah/ehsteh mehs?*
What's on tonight?_____	¿Adónde podríamos ir esta noche? *ahdohndeh pohdreeahmohs eer ehstah nohcheh?*
We want to go to... ____	Nos gustaría ir a... *nohs goostahreeah eer ah...*
Which films are_____ showing?	¿Qué películas dan? *keh pehleekoolahs dahn?*
What sort of film is_____ that?	¿Qué clase de película es? *keh klahseh deh pehleekoolah ehs?*
suitable for everyone ___	para todos los públicos *pahrah tohdohs lohs poobleekohs*
not suitable for _____ children	prohibido para menores de 12/16 años *proheebeedoh pahrah mehnohrehs deh dohtheh/dyehtheesehees ahnyohs*
original version _____	versión original *behrsyohn ohree<u>h</u>eenahl*
subtitled_____	subtitulada *soobteetoolahdah*
dubbed_____	doblada *dohblahdah*

Is it a continuous showing?	¿Es sesión continua?
	ehs sehsyohn kohnteenooah?
What's on at...?	¿Qué dan en...?
	keh dahn ehn...?
– the theatre?	¿Qué dan en el teatro?
	keh dahn ehn ehl tehahtroh?
– the concert hall?	¿Qué dan en la sala de conciertos?
	keh dahn ehn lah sahlah deh kohnthyehrtohs?
– the opera?	¿Qué dan en la ópera?
	keh dahn ehn lah ohpehrah?
Where can I find a good disco around here?	¿Dónde hay una buena discoteca por aquí?
	dohndeh ay oonah bwehnah deeskohtehkah pohr ahkee?
Is it for members only?	¿Hay que ser socio?
	ay keh sehr sohthyoh?
Where can I find a good cabaret club around here?	¿Dónde hay un buen cabaret por aquí?
	dohndeh ay oon bwehn kahbahreh pohr ahkee?
Is it evening wear only?	¿Hay que ir en traje de etiqueta?
	ay keh eer ehn trahheh deh ehteekehtah?
Should I/we dress up?	¿Es recomendable ir en traje de etiqueta?
	ehs rehkohmehndahbleh eer ehn trahheh deh ehteekehtah?
What time does the show start?	¿A qué hora empieza el espectáculo?
	ah keh ohrah ehmpyehthah ehl ehspehktahkooloh?
When's the next soccer match?	¿Cuándo es el próximo partido de fútbol?
	kwahlndoh ehs ehl prohxeemoh pahrteedoh deh footbohl?
Who's playing?	¿Quiénes juegan?
	kyehnehs hwehgahn?

| I'd like an escort for____ tonight. Could you arrange that for me? | Quisiera contratar un/una acompañante para esta noche. ¿Podría hacerme una reserva? |
| | *keesyehrah kohntrahtahr oon/oonah ahkohmpahnyahnteh pahrah ehstah nohcheh. podreeah ahthehrmeh oonah rehsehrbah?* |

11.3 Booking tickets

Could you book some____ tickets for us?	¿Podría hacernos una reserva?
	pohdreeah ahthehrnohs oonah rehsehrbah?
We'd like to book... ____ tickets/a table...	Quisiéramos...entradas/una mesa...
	keesyehrahmohs...ehntrahdahs/oonah mehsah...
– tickets/seats in the ___ stalls	Quisiéramos...entradas en la platea
	keesyehrahmohs...ehntrahdahs ehn lah plahtehah
– tickets/seats on the ___ balcony	Quisiéramos...entradas en el palco
	keesyehrahmohs...ehntrahdahs ehn ehl pahlkoh
– box seats _____	Quisiéramos...entradas en el palco privado
	keesyehrahmohs...ehntrahdahs ehn ehl pahlkoh preebahdoh
– a table at the front ___	Quisiéramos una mesa adelante
	keesyehrahmohs oonah mehsah ahdehlahnteh
– in the middle _____	Quisiéramos una mesa al centro
	keesyehrahmohs oonah mehsah ahl thehntroh

¿Para qué función desea reservar?	Which performance do you want to book for?
¿Qué sector prefiere?	Where would you like to sit?
No hay billetes.	Everything's sold out
Sólo quedan entradas de pie	It's standing room only
Sólo quedan entradas en el palco	We've only got balcony seats left
Sólo quedan entradas en la galería	We've only got seats left in the gallery
Sólo quedan entradas en la platea	We've only got stalls seats left
Sólo quedan entradas adelante	We've only got seats left at the front
Sólo quedan entradas atrás	We've only got seats left at the back
¿Cuántas entradas quiere?	How many seats would you like?
Tiene que retirar las entradas antes de las...	You'll have to pick up the tickets before...o'clock
¿Me permite las entradas?	Tickets, please
Este es su asiento	This is your seat

– at the back _____ Quisiéramos una mesa atrás
keesyehrahmohs oonah mehsah ahtrahs

Could I book...seats ___ ¿Podría reservar...entradas para la
for the...o'clock   función de las...?
performance?   *pohdreeah rehsehrbahr...ehntrahdahs*
                          pahrah lah foonthyohn deh lahs...?

Are there any seats left _ ¿Quedan entradas para esta noche?
for tonight?   *kehdahn ehntrahdahs pahrah ehstah*
                          nohcheh?

How much is a ticket? _ ¿Cuánto sale la entrada?
                          kwahntoh sahleh lah ehntrahdah?

When can I pick the____ tickets up?	¿Cuándo puedo pasar a retirar las entradas?
	kwahndoh pwehdoh pahsahr ah rehteerahr lahs ehntrahdahs?
I've got a reservation____	Tengo una reserva
	tehngoh oonah rehsehrbah
My name's... _____	Me llamo...
	meh lyahmoh...

12 Sports

12.1 Sporting questions 139

12.2 By the waterfront 139

12.3 In the snow 141

12.1 Sporting questions

Where can we... _____ around here?	¿Dónde se puede...? _dohndeh seh pwehdeh...?_
Is there a... _____ around here?	¿Hay algún...por aquí cerca? _ay ahlgoon...pohr ahkee thehrkah?_
Can I hire a...here? _____	¿Alquilan...? _ahlkeelahn...?_
Can I take...lessons? ___	¿Dan clases de...? _dahn klahsehs deh...?_
How much is that per ___ hour/per day/class?	¿Cuánto sale por hora/día/clase? _kwahntoh sahleh pohr ohrah/deeah/klahseh?_
Do I need a permit _____ for that?	¿Se necesita un permiso? _seh nehthehseetah oon pehrmeesoh?_
Where can I get _____ the permit?	¿Dónde se consiguen los permisos? _dohndeh seh kohnseeghehn lohs pehrmeesohs?_

12.2 By the waterfront

Is it a long way to_____ the sea still?	¿Falta mucho para llegar al mar? _fahltah moochoh pahrah lyehgahr ahl mahr?_
Is there a...around _____ here?	¿Hay algún...por aquí? _ay ahlgoon...pohr ahkee?_
– an outdoor/indoor/ ___ public swimming pool	¿Hay alguna piscina por aquí? _ay ahlgoonah peestheenah pohr ahkee?_
– a sandy beach_____	¿Hay alguna playa con arena por aquí? _ay ahlgoonah plahyah kohn ahrehnah pohr ahkee?_
– a nudist beach_____	¿Hay alguna playa nudista por aquí? _ay ahlgoonah plahyah noodeestah pohr ahkee?_
– mooring _____	¿Hay algún atracadero por aquí? _ay ahlgoon ahtrahkahdehroh pohr ahkee?_

Are there any rocks here?	¿Hay rocas?
	ay rohkahs?
When's high/low tide?	¿Cuándo sube/baja la marea?
	kwahndoh soobeh/bahhah lah mahrehah?
What's the water temperature?	¿Qué temperatura tiene el agua?
	keh tehmpehrahtoorah tyehneh ehl ahgwah?
Is it (very) deep here?	¿Es (muy) profundo?
	ehs mwee prohfoondoh?
Can you stand here?	¿Se puede hacer pie?
	seh pwehdeh ahtehr pyeh?
Is it safe to swim here?	¿Es seguro para nadar?
	ehs sehgooroh pahrah nahdahr?
Are there any currents?	¿Hay corriente?
	ay kohrryehnteh?
Are there any rapids/ waterfalls in this river?	¿Este río tiene rápidos/cascadas?
	ehsteh reeoh tyehneh rahpeedohs/kahskahdahs?
What does that flag/ buoy mean?	¿Qué significa aquella bandera/boya?
	keh seegneefeekah ahkehlyah bahndehrah/bohyah?
Is there a life guard on duty here?	¿Hay algún vigilante de servicio?
	ay ahlgoon veeheelante deh sehrbeetheeoh?
Are dogs allowed here?	¿Está permitido traer perros?
	ehstah pehrmeeteedoh trahehr pehrrohs?
Is camping on the beach allowed?	¿Está permitido acampar en la playa?
	ehstah pehrmeeteedoh ahkahmpahr ehn lah plahyah?
Are we allowed to build a fire here?	¿Está permitido hacer fuego?
	ehstah pehrmeeteedoh ahtehr fwehgoh?

Peligro	Prohibido pescar	Prohibido bañarse
Danger	No fishing	No swimming
Aguas de pesca	Prohibido hacer	Permiso obligatorio
Fishing water	surfing No surfing	Permits only

12.3 In the snow

Can I take ski lessons __ here?	¿Dan clases de esquí? *dahn klahsehs deh eskee?*
for beginners/ _____ advanced	para principiantes/avanzados *pahrah preentheepyahntehs/ahbahnthahdohs*
How large are the_____ groups?	¿De cuántas personas son los grupos? *deh kwahntahs pehrsohnahs sohn lohs groopohs?*
What language are_____ the classes in?	¿En qué idioma son las clases? *ehn keh eedyohmah sohn lahs klahsehs?*
I'd like a lift pass, _____ please	Quisiera un pase para las telesillas *keesyehrah oon pahseh pahrah lahs tehlehseelyahs*
Must I give you a _____ passport photo?	¿Se necesita foto? *seh nehthehseetah fohtoh?*
Where can I have a ____ passport photo taken?	¿Dónde puedo sacarme fotos? *dohndeh pwehdoh sahkahrmeh fohtohs?*
Where are the _____ beginners' slopes?	¿Dónde están las pistas para principiantes? *dohndeh ehstahn lahs peestahs pahrah preentheepyahntehs?*
Are there any runs for __ cross-country skiing?	¿Hay pistas de esquí de fondo por aquí? *ay peestahs deh ehskee deh fohndoh pohr ahkee?*
Have the cross _____ -country runs been marked?	¿Las pistas de esquí de fondo están señalizadas? *lahs peestahs deh ehskee deh fohndoh ehstahn sehnyahleethahdahs?*
Are the...in operation?__	¿Están abiertos los...? *ehstahn ahbyehrtohs lohs...?*
– the ski lifts _____	¿Ya funcionan los telesquís? *yah foonthyohnahn lohs tehlehskees?*
– the chair lifts _____	¿Ya funcionan las telesillas? *yah foonthyohnahn lahs tehlehseelyahs?*
Are the slopes usable? _	¿Están abiertas las pistas? *ehstahn ahbyehrtahs lahs peestahs?*

13

Sickness

13.1 Call (fetch) the doctor 143

13.2 Patient's ailments 143

13.3 The consultation 144

13.4 Medication and prescriptions 148

13.5 At the dentist's 149

13.1 Call (fetch) the doctor

Could you call/fetch a __ doctor quickly, please?
¿Podría llamar/ir a buscar rápido a un médico, por favor?
pohdreeah lyahmahr/eer ah booskahr rahpeedoh ah oon mehdeekoh, pohr fahbohr?

When does the doctor _ have surgery?
¿Cuándo tiene consulta el médico?
kwahndoh tyehneh kohnsooltah ehl mehdeekoh?

When can the doctor___ come?
¿Cuándo puede venir el médico?
kwahndoh pwehdeh behneer ehl mehdeekoh?

I'd like to make an _____ appointment to see the doctor
¿Podría pedirme hora con el médico?
pohdreeah pehdeermeh ohrah kohn ehl mehdeekoh?

I've got an _____ appointment to see the doctor at...
Tengo hora con el médico para las...
tehngoh ohrah kohn ehl mehdeekoh pahrah lahs...

Which doctor/chemist __ has night/weekend duty?
¿Qué médico/farmacia está de guardia esta noche/este fin de semana?
keh mehdeekoh/fahrmahthyah ehstah deh gwahrdyah ehstah nohcheh/ehsteh feen deh sehmahnah?

13.2 Patient's ailments

I don't feel well _____
No me siento bien
noh meh syehntoh byehn

I'm dizzy_____
Tengo mareos *tehngoh mahrehohs*

– ill_____
Estoy enfermo *ehstoy ehnfehrmoh*

– sick _____
Tengo náuseas *tehngoh nahoosehahs*

I've got a cold_____
Estoy acatarrado *ehstoy ahkahtahrrahdoh*

It hurts here_____
Me duele aquí *meh dwehleh ahkee*

I've been throwing up __
He devuelto *eh dehbwehltoh*

I've got... _____	Tengo molestias de...
	tehngoh mohlehstyahs deh...
I'm running a _____ temperature of... degrees	Tengo...grados de fiebre
	tehngoh...grahdohs deh fyehbreh
I've been stung by _____ a wasp	Me ha picado una avispa
	meh ah peekahdoh oonah ahbeespah
I've been stung by an __ insect	Me ha picado un insecto
	meh ah peekahdoh oon eensehktoh
I've been bitten by _____ a dog	Me ha mordido un perro
	meh ah mohrdeedoh oon pehrroh
I've been stung by _____ a jellyfish	Me ha picado una medusa
	meh ah peekahdoh oonah mehdoosah
I've been bitten by _____ a snake	Me ha mordido una serpiente
	meh ah mohrdeedoh oonah sehrpyehnteh
I've been bitten by _____ an animal	Me ha picado un insecto
	meh ah peekahdoh oon eensehktoh
I've cut myself _____	Me he cortado *meh eh kohrtahdoh*
I've burned myself _____	Me he quemado *meh eh kehmahdoh*
I've grazed myself _____	Tengo una rozadura
	tehngoh oonah rohthahdoorah
I've had a fall _____	Me he caído *meh eh kaheedoh*
I've sprained my ankle _	Me he torcido el tobillo
	meh eh tohrtheedoh ehl tohbeelyoh
I've come for the _____ morning-after pill	Vengo a que me dé una píldora del día después
	behngoh ah keh meh deh oonah peeldohrah dehl deeah dehspwehs

13.3 The consultation

Patient's medical history

I'm a diabetic _____	Soy diabético *soy deeahbehteekoh*
I have a heart _____ condition	Soy enfermo cardíaco
	soy ehnfehrmoh kahrdeeahkoh

¿Qué molestias tiene?	What seems to be the problem?
¿Cuánto hace que tiene estas molestias?	How long have you had these symptoms?
¿Ha tenido estas molestias anteriormente?	Have you had this trouble before?
¿Qué temperatura tiene?	How high is your temperature?
Desnúdese	Get undressed, please
Desvístase de la cintura para arriba	Strip to the waist, please
Allí puede quitarse la ropa	You can undress there
Descúbrase el brazo izquierdo/derecho	Roll up your left/right sleeve, please
Recuéstese aquí	Lie down here, please
¿Le duele esto?	Does this hurt?
Respire hondo	Breathe deeply
Abra la boca	Open your mouth

I have asthma _____	Soy asmático *soy ahsmahteekoh*
I'm allergic to... _____	Soy alérgico a... *soy ahlehrheekoh ah...*
I'm...months pregnant __	Estoy embarazada de...meses *ehstoy ehmbahrahthadah deh...mehsehs*
I'm on a diet _____	Sigo una dieta *seegoh oonah dyehtah*
I'm on medication/_____ the pill	Tomo medicamentos/la píldora *tohmoh mehdeekahmehntohs/lah peeldohrah*
I've had a heart attack _ once before	He tenido un ataque cardíaco anteriormente *eh tehneedoh oon ahtahkeh kahrdeeahkoh ahntehryohrmehnteh*
I've had a(n)... _____ operation	Me han operado del/de la... *meh ahn ohpehrahdoh dehl/deh lah...*
I've been ill recently_____	He estado enfermo hace poco *eh ehstahdoh ehnfehrmoh ahtheh pohkoh*
I've got an ulcer _____	Tengo una úlcera *tehngoh oonah oolthehrah*
I've got my period _____	Tengo la regla *tehngoh lah rehglah*

¿Padece alguna alergia?	Do you have any allergies?
¿Toma medicamentos?	Are you on any medication?
¿Sigue alguna dieta?	Are you on a diet?
¿Está embarazada?	Are you pregnant?
¿Está vacunado/a contra el tétanos?	Have you had a tetanus injection?

The diagnosis

Is it contagious?	¿Es contagioso? *ehs kohntah<u>h</u>yohsoh?*
How long do I have to stay...?	¿Hasta cuándo tengo que...? *ahstah kwahndoh tehngoh keh...?*
– in bed	¿Hasta cuándo tengo que guardar cama? *ahstah kwahndoh tehngoh keh gwahrdahr kahmah?*
– in hospital	¿Hasta cuándo tengo que quedarme en el hospital? *ahstah kwahndoh tehngoh keh kehdahrmeh ehn ehl ohspeetahl?*
Do I have to go on a special diet?	¿Tengo que seguir alguna dieta? *tehngoh keh sehgheer ahlgoonah dyehtah?*
Am I allowed to travel?	¿Puedo viajar? *pwehdoh byah<u>h</u>ahr?*
Can I make a new appointment?	¿Puedo volver a pedir hora? *pwehdoh bohlbehr ah pehdeer ohrah?*
When do I have to come back?	¿Cuándo tengo que volver? *kwahndoh tehngoh keh bohlbehr?*
I'll come back tomorrow	Vuelvo mañana *bwehlboh mahnyahnah*

| Vuelva mañana/dentro de...días | Come back tomorrow/in...days' time |

No es nada grave	It's nothing serious
Se ha fracturado el/la...	Your...is broken
Se ha contusionado el/la...	You've got a/some bruised...
Se ha desgarrado el/la...	You've got (a) torn...
Tiene una inflamación	You've got an inflammation
Tiene apendicitis	You've got appendicitis
Tiene bronquitis	You've got bronchitis
Tiene una enfermedad venérea	You've got a venereal disease
Tiene gripe	You've got the flu
Ha tenido un ataque al corazón	You've had a heart attack
Tiene una infección virósica/ bacteriana	You've got an infection (viral..., bacterial...)
Tiene una pulmonía	You've got pneumonia
Tiene una úlcera	You've got an ulcer
Se ha distendido un músculo	You've pulled a muscle
Tiene una infección vaginal	You've got a vaginal infection
Tiene una intoxicación alimenticia	You've got food poisoning
Tiene una insolación	You've got sunstroke
Es alérgico a...	You're allergic to...
Está embarazada	You're pregnant
Quisiera hacerle un análisis de sangre/de orina/de materia fecal	I'd like to have your blood/urine/stools tested
Hay que suturar la herida	It needs stitching
Lo/la voy a derivar a un especialista/a un hospital	I'm referring you to a specialist/ sending you to hospital
Tiene que hacerse radiografías	You'll need to have some x-rays taken
Vuelva a tomar asiento en la sala de espera	Could you wait in the waiting room, please?
Hay que operarlo/operarla	You'll need an operation

13.4 Medication and prescriptions

Voy a recetarle unos antibióticos/un jarabe/un calmante/ unos analgésicos	I'm prescribing antibiotics/a mixture/a tranquillizer/pain killers
Tiene que guardar reposo	Have lots of rest
No tiene que salir a la calle	Stay indoors
Tiene que guardar cama	Stay in bed

antes de cada comida before meals	inyecciones injections	tragar entero swallow whole
cápsulas capsules	para uso externo exclusivamente not for internal use	tabletas tablets
diluir en agua dissolve in water		tomar/ingerir take
gotas drops	ungüento ointment	estos medicamentos afectan la capacidad de conducir this medication impairs your driving
cada...horas every...hours	aplicar/embadurnar rub on	
seguir la cura hasta el final finish the course	cucharadas (soperas/ cucharaditas) spoonfuls (tablespoons/tea-spoons)	
durante...días for...days		...vez/veces cada 24 horas ...times a day

How do I take this _____ medicine?	¿Cómo se toman estos medicamentos? *kohmoh seh tohmahn ehstohs mehdeekahmehntohs?*
How many capsules/___ drops/injections/ spoonfuls/tablets each time?	¿Cuántas cápsulas/gotas/inyecciones/ cucharadas/tabletas por vez? *kwahntahs kahpsoolahs/gohtahs/eenyehkthyohnehs/k oochahrahdahs pohr behth?*

How many times _____ a day?	¿Cuántas veces al día? *kwahntahs behthehs ahl deeah?*
I've forgotten my _____ medication. At home I take...	Se me ha olvidado traer los medicamentos. En casa tomo... *seh meh ah olbeedahdoh trahehr lohs mehdeekahmehntohs. ehn kahsah tohmoh...*
Could you make out a _____ prescription for me?	¿Podría hacerme una receta? *pohdreeah ahtehrmeh oonah rehthehtah?*

13.5 At the dentist's

Do you know a good _____ dentist?	¿Me podría recomendar un buen dentista? *meh pohdreeah rehkohmehndahr oon bwehn dehnteestah?*
Could you make a _____ dentist's appointment for me? It's urgent	¿Me podría pedir hora con el dentista? Es urgente *meh pohdreeah pehdeer ohrah kohn ehl dehnteestah? ehs oorhehnteh*
Can I come in today, _____ please?	¿Me podría atender hoy mismo? *meh pohdreeah ahtehndehr oy meesmoh?*
I have (terrible) _____ toothache	Tengo (un terrible) dolor de muelas *tehngoh (oon tehrreebleh) dohlohr deh mwehlahs*
Could you prescribe/ _____ give me a painkiller?	¿Me podría recetar/dar un analgésico? *meh pohdreeah rehthehtahr/dahr oon ahnahlhehseekoh?*
A piece of my tooth _____ has broken off	Se me ha caído un pedazo de un diente *seh meh ah kaheedoh oon pehdahthoh deh oon dyehnteh*
My filling's come out _____	Se me ha salido un empaste *seh meh ah sahleedoh oon ehmpahsteh*
I've got a broken _____ crown	Se me ha roto la corona *seh meh ah rohtoh lah kohrohnah*

I'd like/I don't want a___ local anaesthetic	Quisiera que/no quiero que me ponga anestesia local
	keesyehrah keh/noh kyehroh keh meh pohngah ahnehstehsyah lohkahl
Can you do a _____ makeshift repair job?	¿Me podría hacer un arreglo provisional?
	meh pohdreeah ahthehr oon ahrrehgloh prohbeesyohnahl?
I don't want this tooth__ pulled	No quiero que me extraiga esta muela
	noh kyehroh keh meh ehxtraygah ehstah mwehlah
My dentures are _____ broken. Can you fix them?	Se me ha roto la dentadura postiza ¿Podría arreglármela?
	seh meh ah rohtoh lah dehntahdoorah pohsteethah. pohdreeah arrehglahrmehlah?

¿Qué diente/muela le duele?	Which tooth hurts?
Tiene un absceso	You've got an abscess
Tengo que tratarle el nervio	I'll have to do a root canal
Voy a ponerle anestesia local	I'm giving you a local anaesthetic
Tengo que empastarle/extraerle/pulirle este/esta...	I'll have to fill/pull this tooth/file this...down
Tengo que usar el torno	I'll have to drill
Abra la boca	Open wide, please
Cierre la boca	Close your mouth, please
Enjuáguese	Rinse, please
¿Le sigue doliendo?	Does it hurt still?

14

In trouble

14.1 Asking for help 152

14.2 Loss 153

14.3 Accidents 153

14.4 Theft 155

14.5 Missing person 155

14.6 The police 156

14.1 Asking for help

English	Spanish
Help!	¡Socorro! *sohkohrroh!*
Fire!	¡Fuego! *fwehgoh!*
Police!	¡Policía! *pohleetheeah!*
Quick!	¡Rápido! *rahpeedoh!*
Danger!	¡Peligro! *pehleegroh!*
Watch out!	¡Cuidado! *kweedahdoh!*
Stop!	¡Alto! *ahltoh!*
Be careful!	¡Cuidado! *kweedahdoh!*
Don't!	¡No, no! *noh, noh!*
Let go!	¡Suelte! *swehlteh!*
Stop that thief!	¡Al ladrón! *ahl lahdrohn!*
Could you help me, please?	¿Podría ayudarme, por favor? *pohdreeah ahyoodahrmeh, pohr fahbohr?*
Where's the police station/emergency exit/fire escape?	¿Dónde está la comisaría/la salida de emergencia/la escalera de incendios? *dohndeh ehstah lah kohmeesahreeah/lah sahleedah deh ehmehrhehnthyah/lah ehskahlehrah deh eenthehndyohs?*
Where's the nearest fire extinguisher?	¿Dónde hay un extintor? *dohndeh ay oon ehxteentohr?*
Call the fire brigade!	¡Llamen a los bomberos! *lyahmehn ah lohs bohmbehrohs!*
Call the police!	¡Llamen a la policía! *lyahmehn ah lah pohleetheeah!*
Call an ambulance!	¡Llamen a una ambulancia! *lyahmehn ah oonah ahmboolahnthyah!*
Where's the nearest phone?	¿Dónde hay un teléfono? *dohndeh ay oon tehlehfohnoh?*
Could I use your phone?	¿Podría llamar por teléfono? *pohdreeah lyahmahr pohr tehlehfohnoh?*
What's the emergency number?	¿Cuál es el número de urgencias? *kwahl ehs ehl noomehroh deh oorhehnthyahs?*

What's the number for the police?	¿Cuál es el número de la policía? _kwahl ehs ehl noomehroh deh lah pohleetheeah?_

14.2 Loss

I've lost my purse/ wallet	Se me ha perdido el monedero/la cartera _seh meh ah pehrdeedoh ehl mohnehdehroh/lah kahrtehrah_
I left my...behind yesterday	Ayer me dejé el/la... _ahyehr meh dehheh ehl/lah..._
I left my...here	Me he dejado el/la...aquí _meh eh dehhahdoh ehl/lah...ahkee_
Did you find my...?	¿Han encontrado mi...? _ahn ehnkohntrahdoh mee...?_
It was right here	Estaba aquí _ehstahbah ahkee_
It's quite valuable	Es muy valioso _ehs mwee bahlyohsoh_
Where's the lost property office?	¿Dónde está la oficina de objetos perdidos? _dohndeh ehstah lah ohfeetheenah deh ohbhehtohs pehrdeedohs?_

14.3 Accidents

There's been an accident	Ha habido un accidente _ah ahbeedoh oon ahktheedehnteh_
Someone's fallen into the water	Se ha caído alguien al agua _seh ah kaheedoh ahlgyehn ahl ahgwah_
There's a fire	Hay un incendio _ay oon eenthehndyoh_
Is anyone hurt?	¿Hay algún herido? _ay ahlgoon ehreedoh?_

Some people have been/ no one's been injured	(No) hay heridos *(noh) ay ehreedohs*
There's someone in ___ the car/train still	Todavía queda alguien en el coche/tren *tohdahbeeah kehdah ahlgyehn ehn ehl kohcheh/trehn*
It's not too bad. Don't __ worry	No es grave. No se preocupe *noh ehs grahbeh. noh seh prehohkoopeh*
Leave everything the ___ way it is, please	No toque nada *noh tohkeh nahdah*
I want to talk to the ___ police first	Primero quisiera hablar con la policía *preemehroh keesyehrah ahblahr kohn lah pohleetheeah*
I want to take a_____ photo first	Primero quisiera sacar una foto *preemehroh keesyehrah sahkahr oonah fohtoh*
Here's my name _____ and address	Aquí tiene mi nombre y dirección *ahkee tyehneh mee nohmbreh ee deerehkthyohn*
Could I have your_____ name and address?	¿Me da su nombre y dirección? *meh dah soo nohmbreh ee deerehkthyohn?*
Could I see some _____ identification/your insurance papers?	¿Me permite su carnet de identidad/sus papeles del seguro? *meh pehrmeeteh soo kahrneh deh eedehnteedahdh/soos pahpehlehs dehl sehgooroh?*
Will you act as a_____ witness?	¿Le importaría hacer de testigo? *leh eempohrtahreeah ahthehr deh tehsteegoh?*
I need the details for ___ the insurance	Necesito los datos para el seguro *nehthehseetoh lohs dahtohs pahrah ehl sehgooroh*
Are you insured? _____	¿Está asegurado? *ehstah ahsehgoorahdoh?*
Third party or _____ comprehensive?	¿Responsabilidad civil o contra todo riesgo? *rehspohnsahbeeleedahdh theebeel oh kohntrah tohdoh ryehsgoh?*

Could you sign here, ___   Firme aquí, por favor
  please?   *feermeh ahkee, pohr fahbohr*

14.4 Theft

I've been robbed _____   Me han robado *meh ahn rohbahdoh*
My...has been stolen ___   Me han robado el/la...
                            meh ahn rohbahdoh ehl/lah...
My car's been _____   Me han abierto el coche
  broken into   *meh ahn ahbyehrtoh ehl kohcheh*

14.5 Missing person

I've lost my child/_____   Se ha perdido mi hijo/mi hija/mi abuela
  grandmother   *seh ah pehrdeedoh mee eehoh/mee*
                            eehah/mee ahbwehlah

Could you help me ____   ¿Podría ayudarme a buscarlo/la?
  find him/her?   *pohdreeah ahyoodahrmeh ah*
                           booskahrloh/lah?

Have you seen a _____   ¿Ha visto a un niño pequeño/a una niña
  small child?   pequeña?
                           ah veestoh ah oon neenyoh
                           pehkehnyoh/ah oonah neenyah
                           pehkehnyah?

He's/she's...years old __   Tiene...años
                            tyehneh...ahnyohs

He's/she's got _____   Tiene el pelo
  short/long/blond/red/   corto/largo/rubio/rojo/castaño/negro/
  brown/black/   canoso/rizado/liso/crespo
  grey/curly/   *tyehneh ehl pehloh/ kohrtoh*
  straight/frizzy hair   */lahrgoh/roobyoh/kahstahnyoh/neh*
                             groh/kahnohsoh/reethahdoh/leesoh/krehs
                             poh

with a ponytail _____   con cola de caballo
                            kohn kohlah deh kahbahlyoh

with plaits _____	con trenzas
	kohn trehnthahs
in a bun _____	con moño *kohn mohnyoh*
He's/she's got_____	Tiene ojos azules/marrones/verdes
blue/brown/green eyes	*tyehneh oh<u>h</u>ohs*
	ahthoolehs/mahrrohnehs/behrdehs
He's wearing _____	Lleva bañador/botas de montaña
swimming trunks/	*lyehbah bahnyahdohr/bohtahs deh*
mountaineering boots	*mohntahnyah*
with/without glasses/ __	con/sin gafas/bolso
a bag	*kohn/seen gahfahs/bohlsoh*
tall/short_____	alto/bajito
	ahltoh/bah<u>h</u>eetoh
This is a photo of _____	Esta es su foto
him/her	*ehstah ehs soo fohtoh*
He/she must be lost ___	Seguramente se habrá perdido
	sehgoorahmehnteh seh ahbrah
	pehrdeedoh

14.6 The police

An arrest

Los papeles del coche, por favor	Your registration papers, please
Conducía demasiado rápido	You were speeding
Tiene mal aparcado el coche	You're not allowed to park here
No ha puesto monedas en el parquímetro	You haven't put money in the meter
No le funcionan los faros	Your lights aren't working
Le vamos a poner una multa de...euros	That's a...euros fine
¿Va a pagar la multa en el acto?	Do you want to pay on the spot?
Tiene que pagar en el acto	You'll have to pay on the spot

I don't speak Spanish __	No hablo español
	noh ahbloh ehspahnyohl
I didn't see the sign ____	No he visto el cartel
	noh eh beestoh ehl kahrtehl
I don't understand _____ what it says	No entiendo lo que dice
	noh ehntyehndoh loh keh deeteh
I was only doing... _____ kilometres an hour	Sólo iba a...kilómetros por hora
	sohloh eebah ah...keelohmehtrohs pohr ohrah
I'll have my car _____ checked	Haré revisar el coche
	ahreh rehbeesahr ehl kohcheh
I was blinded by_____ oncoming lights	Me cegó un coche que venía de frente
	meh thehgoh oon kohcheh keh behneeah deh frehnteh

At the police station

I want to report a _____ collision/missing person/rape	Vengo a hacer la denuncia de un choque/un extravío/una violación
	behngoh ah ahthehr lah dehnoonthyah deh oon chohkeh/oon ehxtrahbeeoh/oonah beeohlahthyohn
Could you make out ___ a report, please?	¿Podría hacer un atestado?
	pohdreeah ahthehr oon ahtehstahdoh?
Could I have a copy ___ for the insurance?	¿Me podría dar una copia para el seguro?
	meh pohdreeah dahr oonah kohpyah pahrah ehl sehgooroh?
I've lost everything_____	He perdido todo
	eh pehrdeedoh tohdoh
I'd like an interpreter ___	Quisiera un intérprete
	keesyehrah oon eentehrprehteh
I'm innocent _____	Soy inocente
	soy eenohthehnteh
I don't know anything __ about it	No sé nada
	noh seh nahdah

I want to speak to ____ someone...	Quisiera hablar con alguien de... *keesyehrah ahblahr kohn ahlgyehn deh...*
from the British _____ consulate	Quisiera hablar con alguien del Consulado Británico *keesyehrah ahblahr kohn ahlgyehn dehl kohnsoolahdoh breetahneekoh*
I need to see someone _ from the British embassy	Quisiera hablar con alguien de la Embajada Británica *keesyehrah ahblahr kohn ahlgyehn deh lah ehmbahhahdah breetahneekah*
I want a lawyer who____ speaks English	Quisiera un abogado que hable inglés *keesyehrah oon ahbohgahdoh keh ahbleh eenglehs*

¿Dónde ha sido?	Where did it happen?
¿Qué se le ha perdido?	What's missing?
¿Qué le han robado?	What's been taken?
¿Me permite su documento de identidad?	Could I see some identification?
¿A qué hora ocurrió?	What time did it happen?
¿Quiénes estuvieron implicados?	Who was involved?
¿Hay testigos?	Are there any witnesses?
Rellene este formulario	Fill this out, please
Firme aquí, por favor	Sign here, please
¿Quiere un intérprete?	Do you want an interpreter?